Children Aloud!

Children Aloud!

Gordon and Ronni Lamont

Illustrations by Martin Cater

NATIONAL SOCIETY/CHURCH HOUSE PUBLISHING

National Society/Church House Publishing,
Church House,
Great Smith Street,
London SW1P 3NZ

ISBN 0 7151 4891 5

Published 1997 by the National Society/Church House Publishing

© *Gordon and Ronni Lamont 1997*

Illustrations © *Martin Cater*

Acknowledgements

Scottish Episcopal Church, *Scottish Liturgy 1982* (p.56)

Sheila Forsdyke © 1996 ('The boy who saw Easter', p.60)

Cover design by Julian Smith

Printed in England by The Cromwell Press, Melksham, Wiltshire

Contents

Photocopiable pages are listed here in italics

Contents

Introduction

What do we mean by all-age worship?

Jim was four years old. It was the day of his Nursery School Harvest Festival and a visiting vicar was giving a talk.

'Here's two lovely rosy red apples,' said the vicar, picking up some fruit from the display. Jim's hand shot up at once, but the vicar wasn't taking any interruptions and ploughed on.

'But, but . . .', interrupted Jim, then, 'Excuse me . . .'

The vicar ignored him. The assembled parents didn't. We could all see what Jim could see – one of those 'rosy red apples' was bright green without the slightest hint of red. Jim simply wanted to tell him that – he'd probably been doing colours at Nursery that week. The vicar kept going, Jim kept interrupting, the vicar kept ignoring him, the parents were splitting their sides and the point of the talk was lost!

That's not the only religious event that Jim's sabotaged, but those are other stories.

Of course the Nursery Harvest was not intended to be 'all-age', it was aimed at the very youngest children, but the lesson that vicar should have learnt is relevant to all worship where children are present; plan with children in mind and respond to their needs. This is simply because whilst adults can appreciate and learn from material aimed at children, children can rarely reciprocate. On the whole, that which is aimed at adults will leave children bored, then restless, then difficult, then disruptive. We have often heard it said that children can appreciate the colour and smells and sound of adult worship, that they should be left to 'soak it up' and that in time they will learn to appreciate its mystery. On the whole we find this view unconvincing. If it were so, our churches would be full of children gazing in awe and sitting peacefully through wordy services. If this were the best way to learn, school lessons would be like university lectures, and there would be no such thing as children's cinema, or children's books, TV, or radio. In every area of life we target the age group. It is not good enough to plonk children in the midst of an adult service and expect them to appreciate it.

Perhaps then, our church services should become little more than kindergarten sessions of children-centred worship? It can be argued that occasionally they should, but only occasionally. Our concept of all-age worship recognizes:

❖   that children need to exercise their own spirituality;

❖   that children do not attend church merely to learn how to behave in church;

❖   that it is good for adults and children to worship together;

- ✦   that adults can learn from children and that the converse is true;
- ✦   that at times adults and children will work, learn and worship separately;
- ✦   that children's voices should be heard in the worshipping community;
- ✦   that adults also need to be spiritually fed.

In this book you will find a variety of material which is our attempt to work out a concept of all-age worship in practice. The book includes:

- ✦   prayers, readings and drama prepared by children then shared with the whole church;
- ✦   prayers which the whole church works on together;
- ✦   drama and readings for children and adults to do together;
- ✦   raps for children (and perhaps adults) to perform to the whole church;
- ✦   sample talk and service outlines for all age worship;
- ✦   pew sheets for use during services;

It will be noted that there is an emphasis on children speaking within services – in readings, prayers and drama. When we say that children's voices should be heard, we mean it quite literally because so many words in church are written for and spoken by adults. We want to redress this balance. We recognize, however, that for many children solo speaking is inappropriate, so we offer choral raps, and dramas of varying complexity.

Pew sheets are often seen as 'something to keep them quiet', and although we recognize that there are times when children need to be quiet during more adult parts of a service or because it is good for children to experience the spirituality of silence, we encourage you to feed the results of the pew sheets into the service at a later point. Many are designed with this in mind. A number of the drama pieces are intended to be rehearsed and then presented in church and lend themselves to adults and children working together. It is a feature of this book that we greatly value these types of shared experience.

We're finding our way in this area as is everyone else, so all the material is offered in a spirit of experiment. It's all open to adaptation and refinement. We do ask, however, that if you perform any of the plays in this book, you credit the authors in any publicity material or handout. That proviso aside, take it and make it fit your situation and needs. In the next section we explore some possibilities for doing so.

Designing the liturgy

Designing an all-age liturgy – a service of worship – is perhaps one of the most difficult things that we ever do in planning worship. A service has many possible aims, and working these out should be your first activity. Some people's brains seize up if you ask them what their aims are, or what the theology behind an idea is, or even the simplest question of all: 'Why?' So it might be a good idea to work out your aims as a group, or at least over a cup of coffee with someone else. If you start with a brainstorming session, you should come up with enough to guide you in the creative act of giving birth to the service.

Some examples of aims, in no particular order:

◆   to bring people together;

◆   to enable the whole congregation to engage with an idea (e.g. families) in the life of the Church;

◆   to enable people to pray more clearly about a subject area;

◆   to share a story from the Bible;

◆   to imagine what something was like (e.g. to be there when a blind man was given back his sight);

◆   to worship God together as individuals and families within the larger family of the Church;

◆   to consider how we pray;

◆   to give a secure environment in which children can grow in their faith.

The list could be as long as this book, and a bit longer. The art is to identify your aims for this particular act of worship, and then hold them in view.

Once you have your aims, we suggest handing over to one person. A committee is not, in our experience, a good forum for working out the nuts and bolts. Send off a volunteer, give them a set period of time – perhaps about a week – and then reconvene to see what they've come up with.

If you are that lucky person we suggest the following as a workable approach to devising the service:

Resources

Gather up your resources. There are lots of books available. Responses and prayers need not come from books aimed at children, since we are aiming at a balanced structure which offers something for everyone. The very act of joining in a short prayer can be immensely valuable.

Some books which we recommend are:

> *The Promise of his Glory*, CHP, 1991
>
> *Lent, Holy Week, Easter*, CUP/CHP/SPCK, 1984
>
> *Patterns for Worship*, CHP, 1995

These have been through General Synod and are authorized for use in Anglican churches. We find that there are sometimes too many words (rather like Mozart's notes) for genuine all-age worship, so careful selection is important.

The Iona community's worship book is excellent. It is *The Pattern of our Days*, Wild Goose Publications, 1996.

The Alternative Service Book 1980 (the ASB) is also full of useful collects, readings and prayers which you can take and adapt. It has a useful guide to the themes for the ASB services, which can be found on page 1092.

There are many 'Office' prayer books available too. We enjoy the *Celtic Daily Office* (by A. Raine and J. T. Skinner, Marshall Pickering, 1994) enormously, and it has a wide variety of prayers and readings that you can adapt. We also value *The Rhythm of Life* by David Adam (Triangle, 1996). Celtic spirituality has a great deal to offer all-age worship. To those who don't know its strengths and depths, Celtic spirituality can appear to embrace the spirit of the age rather than the fullness of Christianity. But true Celtic Christianity is rooted deeply in Trinitarian belief. Many prayers of the tradition speak directly of the work of God the Father, Son and Holy Spirit. It is Christian through and through. God is immanent in this way of thinking – not to be striven for, but to be realized as just out of our sight but very close by – ' 'tis only the splendour of light hideth thee'. God is also caught up in the intimate details of our life, and frequently comes to us as a stranger, hence the Celtic emphasis on hospitality. This is an approach which many are finding helpful as they explore their own spirituality.

Scripture Union have an excellent, and very imaginative, book on prayer: *101 Ideas for Creative Prayers (for group use)*, by Judith Morell, Scripture Union, 1995.

In the new three-year lectionary *The Christian Year: Calendar, Lectionary and Collects* (Church House Publishing, 1997) there is a wide range of Bible stories covered, so you are likely to find something suitable for people of all-ages to explore. A more mixed blessing is that the material is not organized under themes; rather the readings are left to speak for themselves. On the whole we feel that this is positive because it allows you to choose an appropriate theme, and the same readings might suggest a different theme for an evening service to that which you will choose for morning all-age worship. The key goals, of course, are the same as for all worship planning, but we believe that the greater flexibility offered by the new lectionary, in conjunction with other resources, offers enhanced opportunities for integrated worship and teaching.

Surround yourself with as many books as you can cope with, dip into them and mark all the pieces that you think are relevant to your theme. Pick too many hymns/songs on the theme, so that these can be whittled down later. Then you have to commit pen to paper, or fingers to keyboard, and begin to put the service together.

Structure

We'll assume that this service is to include hymns/songs, prayers, readings and a talk/activity session. In other words, it is to follow a form which most churchgoers will be able to recognize as worship. There are many possible structures available here. We give what seems to work best for us. As always, adapt and improve!

We like to start with a **Bible verse** as a call to worship. The ASB is good at those – look under your theme, if it's covered, and see what is recommended, then see if a different translation of the Bible expresses it in a more 'user friendly' form.

Then we'd put in a **hymn** or song. This draws the people together, and helps them relax. It's not going to be too radical – church always starts like this!

That's the easy bit. Now you come to the meat/nut cutlet of the day: what is most appropriate next? We suggest some responses, or a **prayer** (the Collect for that day's theme?) leading into the **Lord's Prayer**. Note, however, that these need not be dry and wordy. The form of prayer could follow one of the interactive suggestions in this book. A communally read prayer will include a large section of the congregation if it uses simple enough words for primary age children to join in.

Follow this with either another song, or the **reading**. You need to let everyone know just what you are thinking about, and you have to reinforce the message. They won't catch on as quickly as you do – you wrote the service!

You will have to make a decision about whether the whole church stays together throughout the service. You may choose to split at some point to follow different **activities** before recombining.

We strongly recommend that if children are staying in with the adults, the reading and talk/activity or combination come early on in the service. This is the high concentration part for the children (and adults, but we expect more of them) so it needs to come early.

The reading can take many forms, from a rehearsed reading to a simple drama, or an instant 'everybody join in' session.

It is probably a good idea to have some sort of **movement** at this point, to kill the fidgets: sing an action song, or hold a simple procession.

If everyone is in together, this is a good point for the **talk**. See hints below for how to keep this interesting for young children but don't forget to throw the odd question/comment out to the adults as well, or they'll lose interest.

Remember, however, that a talk is not always necessary. A drama, dance or reading can be constructed to be entirely self-explanatory or leave enough mystery to get young and old asking questions which you may answer or leave hanging in the air.

If you have an activity that involves drawing/craft type work, be absolutely clear as to the logistics of how to move from talk to activity with the minimum of fuss. This could be the point at which children do one thing (a craft or drawing activity growing out of the talk) and the adults have their point of focus. You might choose to move the children (or adults!) into another space, or have the two activities running concurrently in the same space. Either way, the logistics need careful planning.

At the end of this part all sorts of things may happen; you may wish to use the created items as an offertory, or you may stop to sing a hymn. You may mount the items on a specially prepared display . . . the list is endless. But you need to know how you pull all the congregation back into relative order, to continue with the liturgy.

We recommend **prayers** after the activity session. The children will have moved, thought, used their hands and will be getting tired. So be creative as to how you pray. You'll find a number of ideas in this book. Use responses wherever you can – most of the congregation can join in, and it catches people back together again.

And so we move towards the **end**. Don't worry if there seems very little on your plan. We are aiming at 40–45 minutes, and it whizzes by. End with a hymn/song and perhaps dismissing responses, and wipe your fevered brow.

Your service outline, for a service where all stay together, might look something like this:

1. **Opening responses** – written by you/your team or from a book.
2. **Hymn** – something lively and easy for all ages to join in.
3. **Introduction** to theme – Two/three minutes. Probably question and answer involving children.
4. **Bible reading** – could be dramatized or spread between readers. Keep it short and clear.
5. **Hymn** – reflecting theme/reading if possible or could be a simple song which the children have practised and now teach to the whole congregation.
6. **Talk** – with children at front.
7. **Statement of faith** if no baptism at service. Children could be doing their own activity (such as pew sheets or something you asked them to draw/write/think about at the end of the talk).
8. **Prayers** involving children (or baptism).
9. **Lord's Prayer**.
10. **Hymn**.
11. **Closing responses** and blessing.

The above offers lots for children to do but without the whole service being focused on their needs alone.

Patterns for Worship gives the authorized basic structures for A Service of the Word as follows:

A Service of the Word

The preparation

1. The minister welcomes the people with a **liturgical greeting**.

2. **Authorized Prayers of Penitence** are used here or in *The prayers*.

3. *Venite*, *Kyries*, *Gloria*, a hymn, song, or a set of responses may be used.

4. The **Collect** is said here or at section 9.

The ministry of the Word

This includes

5. **Readings (or a Reading) from Holy Scripture.**

6. **A psalm** or, if occasion demands, a scriptural song.

7. **A sermon.**

8. **An authorized creed**, or, if occasion demands, an authorized **affirmation of faith.**

The prayers

These include

9. **Intercessions and thanksgivings.**

10. **The Lord's Prayer.**

The conclusion

11. The service concludes with a **liturgical ending.**

You will find that you keep adjusting the liturgy as the days go by. Read it aloud, as it is always different like that, and be ruthless if it's got too many words – God's Holy Spirit needs some space to act too.

Now share your service. Listen to what others say. Change it as you feel you should. Then allocate parts and do it.

After the service, it often helps to have a debriefing. How could it have been better? What went well? What are the particular skills of your leaders, and how can they be better utilized? Was it good as worship, or was it entertainment alone?

Refer back to your aims at every point, and decide if the service met them. If it did, you should be writing this book!

Integrating all-age ideas with eucharistic services

Many of the ideas in this book will work equally well in both non-eucharistic and eucharistic services, but we recognize that Eucharists can create special tensions for all-age worship, for reasons such as:

- the perceived need of some members of the congregation for a peaceful and reflective time;
- long, wordy services;
- complicated concepts within the eucharistic prayers;
- a set structure with little room for manoeuvre.

The obvious places where ideas from this book can be used are in the Ministry of the Word and the Intercessions. There are numerous examples of each of these, such as:

Ministry of the Word

- Nativity plays, pp. 20–21 and 22–6
- The Tale of the Wise Ones, pp. 32–6
- Candlemas talk outline, pp. 41–2
- Family drama and talk, pp. 46 and 49
- Suffering talk, pp. 52–4
- Easter tableaux, pp. 56–7 and 63
- Rogation talk outlines, pp. 70–73
- Pentecost pageant, pp. 76–7
- The Parable of the Two House Builders drama, pp. 84–7
- Talents and Sower dramas, pp. 90 and 93–6
- Harvest talk, pp. 91–2

Prayers

- Christmas tree prayers, p. 12
- Crib Service outline, pp. 27–8
- Candlemas prayers, p. 42
- Family tree prayers, pp. 44–5
- Prayers focusing on suffering, pp. 52–4
- Rogation talk outlines, pp. 70–73
- Remembrance prayers, pp. 100–103

If you wish to be more adventurous, you could consider using one of the Raps in place of a hymn.

The main aim, as in planning any worship which involves children, should be to consider how the service will look and feel to them. A eucharistic service in which the children stay with the adults could be made more child-friendly by including the following:

✦   songs/hymns – well known and enjoyed by children (replace one with a rap?);

✦   Ministry of the Word – an all-age reading/drama/talk;

✦   Intercessions – involving children as above;

✦   Eucharistic Prayer – choose the shortest you can find and give the children pew sheets to use during this part of the service;

✦   before the final hymn – look at and comment on the children's pew sheets.

A service in which the children leave at some point to do their own activities could include some of the above elements as appropriate.

Tips for talks

Worship leaders can learn from primary school teachers:

Have an area near the front where the children can gather, to sit and listen and interact during any input. This 'sitting on the carpet' brings the children right up under the leader's eye. They know they are being talked to – there is plenty of eye contact and questions; names are used. We usually just get them to come and sit, on any space immediately in front of the worship leader – be it near the communion rail, in a space at the front of the church or wherever. The effect of this is that many children go into a different behaviour mode, learned at school and transferred to church. They understand that they are being addressed specifically and that they should listen and take part.

The next is obvious from the above – learn some names and use them! Learn the children's names faster than the parents' – they are used to being referred to as Beth's Mum or Dad; learn Beth's name and they'll wait to introduce themselves later.

Make eye contact with the children as you speak to them. Watch any teacher at work: their eyes move all the time, and hold the children's attention. You'll also pick up the first signs of flagging interest if you are watching them closely.

Don't ignore tinies who insist on talking to you – remember Jim and the Nursery Harvest as related in our opening paragraph! At a recent crib service, Ronni had a tot who chattered all the way through; children don't mind you quietly saying 'Really?' or 'Yes' to such a child. They come across them daily at school! So Ronni said the odd word to this little girl, and she was happy.

Children (and adults) have short concentration spans. Don't talk for long.

Use visual aids.

Make the talk interactive: ask questions, show things, ask for responses in movement – responding with you, acting out the story etc.

Take them for a walk if the talk is long: it gets rid of fidgets. You could go to a different part of the building to illustrate a point, or even build in a basic procession. They won't mind moving – it's the adults who like the security of a pew!

Most important of all, keep the concepts simple. They may be able to tell you that Jesus came to save us from our sins, but ask them what it means and you may discover that they've got interesting notions . . . Don't teach jargon, teach appropriate spirituality.

Photocopiable sheets

We have grouped all the explanatory material at the beginning of each section. The pages at the end of each section are photocopiable and these are distinguished by decorative borders (e.g. Advent and Christmas on p. 18).

Pew sheets

At the back of this book you will find photocopiable pew sheets. These are based around many of the same themes as the sections in the main part of the book. They can be used during those parts of the service where there is a more adult focus. On the whole we are not in favour of 'things to keep the children quiet' so although the pew sheets contain some traditional style puzzles for amusement, the bulk of the ideas are creative and require the users to engage with the theme and issues of the service. For this reason, we suggest that the children's work on pew sheets is referred to and looked at later in the service.

And finally . . .

Do we really value children equally with adults? If we did, perhaps we'd:

- ✦ Let the children have the run of the main building while the adults went in to the 'Sunday Club room' for their activities . . .

- ✦ Employ the professional to teach the children and use a volunteer for the adults.

- ✦ Design or redesign our churches with appropriate area/furniture for all-ages.

- ✦ Produce less wordy services.

- ✦ Ensure that every service had a small section especially for the grown-ups.

Advent and Christmas

Prayers for Advent and Christmas

Christmas tree prayers

Age range:	All age
Materials:	Wallpaper or large sheets of paper
	A4 sheets, crayons and pencils
Working space:	In church as part of service

Create a large Christmas tree drawing out of wallpaper and have this fixed in a prominent position before the service begins.

Position paper and drawing/writing materials at the end of pews/rows before service begins.

At the point of the prayers in the service, talk with the children and adults about things which we have to be thankful for at Christmas time. During some music allow time for children and adults to draw or write their responses. At the end of this time show everyone how to draw a simple cross shape on the back of the paper to make it look like a parcel tied with string. End this section of the prayers with a simple prayer of thanksgiving, thanking God for all that we enjoy at this time of year.

Finally invite a couple of children to collect the prayers and, during the next part of the service, to stick them on the tree, parcel side out, with Blu-tack to form a reminder of all that we have to be thankful for.

Choral prayer

Age range:	All age
Materials:	None
Working space:	In church as part of service or during Sunday Club

This is a simple, adaptable form of prayer which relies on the repeated phrase, 'Joy, joy to the world'.

In church

Practise the choral response a few times and then introduce simple one-line prayers to fit the rhythm. An example is given on page 18. You could rehearse different groups or individuals to take various lines of the prayer. To integrate the prayer into a talk, you could ask for suggestions for the lines during the talk and discuss them.

In Sunday Club

Another approach was used at St Peter's, Hemel Hempstead, Sunday Club in January 1997. A basic form of the prayers with gaps was introduced and the children added their own responses. These were pooled and discussed until one final version was agreed. The lines were split between individuals with all the children joining in the chorus. The prayer was then used in church when we rejoined the main worship. Afterwards one member of the congregation suggested that if the response were taught to everyone, it could become a prayer for the whole church to join in with. The finished form of the prayer from St Peter's is given on page 18.

Christmas rap

Introduction

Raps and simple poems can be particularly useful in worship where children are involved. The repetitive rhythm makes it easy for a wide age range to join in and helps children to learn the words or make up their own. In many ways this kind of activity is similar to traditional chanting and shares the advantage that the sound can carry a long way. The introduction of this kind of highly rhythmic material can form a counterpoint and contrast to other spoken and sung parts of the service.

Like all the raps in this book, the one on page 19 can be rehearsed by children in their own session and then presented to the whole church when everyone joins together. It can also be used as a basis for children writing their own raps. Aim for a sharp, clear delivery. To maintain interest, if you have a large enough group, you could split the verses between smaller groups. You could also use a rhythm backing from a tape or keyboard.

You could rehearse this rap the week before and use it at the start of a service since it raises the question, 'What's so special about Jesus?'

Age range:	7–12. The age range will depend on how the idea is developed; teenagers might like to perform their own raps with accompaniment.
Working space:	Space in which to prepare away from the main church – could be quite noisy!

Christmas – All-age Nativity plays

Introduction

It's Christmas again! How can you present the well-known story in a way which will encourage people to think, ask questions and take a fresh look? The simple scripted dramas in this section provide some answers. There are two plays in this section (see below) and a third under Epiphany on page 30. They can be adapted, expanded and revised to suit different groups, ages, buildings and congregations. They are all designed to be rehearsed beforehand, so will require a fair amount of adult input.

Nativity play

The script for this can be found on pages 20–21. This is simplest of the Nativity plays, using narration and movement, with most speaking parts requiring only one or two lines to be learned.

There are three movement journey sequences: Mary and Joseph, Shepherds, Wise Men. They are meant to happen to music and take each group on a journey around parts of the church (so that mums and dads can get a good look!). The music can be pre-recorded or supplied by a music group; it could be (as in the script) organ music; or you could sing carols at the appropriate points. A really musical church could attempt a mixture of all these styles!

Age range:	The original production, at St Peter's Church, St Albans, was at Christmas 1993, and involved the Sunday Club – with older members taking the more taxing roles. This piece would work with a mixture of ages, since there is plenty of movement for the very young and some more humorous parts for older children or adults.
Working space:	This play needs a reasonable performance space (dependent on the size of the cast), and good sight lines if possible. There are parts which involve the cast in processing around the church.

Characters

Messenger	Needs to be a strong reader (*can all be read from scroll*). Can be in the pulpit so could be miked. M or F.
Mary	3 lines.
Narrator	Needs to be a strong reader (*can all be read from scroll*). Could be at lectern so could be miked. M or F.
Joseph	2 lines.
Two Innkeepers	Mime only.

Innkeeper 3	One speech.
Angel	One line.
Shepherd 1	One line.
Shepherds	Mime journey.
Star	One line.
Wise Man	Speaks simple poem.
Two other Wise Men	Mime journey.

Shepherds' play

The script for this can be found on pages 22–6. This Nativity play was originally produced at St Peter's Church, St Albans, Christmas 1995. It uses some elements of traditional Nativity plays, mixed with more contemporary references. These references are bound to date, so feel free to eject or upgrade them – they couldn't be more corny than at present!

Age range:	Mixed. This would work well as a genuine all age piece with adults and children working alongside one another. There are very simple lines which can be shared out amongst the youngest children, as well as slightly more complex Narrator roles.
Working space:	This play needs a reasonable performance space (dependent on the size of the cast), and good sight lines if possible.

Production notes

The play is designed so that it can, for the most part, be rehearsed in groups.

The Shepherds are probably best suited to the younger children with some older children and adults amongst them for support. Shepherd 1 is the lead shepherd and there are two character parts, originally designed to suit the abilities of particular children – The Old Shepherd, and The Cool Shepherd.

In the original production, the Angels were Brownie Guides – rehearsed separately – thus the 'jokes' about badges!

Another separate rehearsal group could be the Narrators who need to be good readers – they can read the script from the pulpit and lectern if appropriate.

Each of these groups can be expanded by extra characters joining in the 'All' speeches, by splitting the lines between more characters, and by adding simple movement as appropriate.

We rehearsed for four sessions in Sunday Club and Brownies with two full runs-through in the days before the service.

Characters

Shepherds There's room for great flexibility here to expand the number of shepherds if needed, to have a mix of ages and to tailor the individual lines to different participants. You could, for example, have a musical shepherd, a jokey shepherd, a know-all shepherd (the Vicar?) . . .

Narrators 1 & 2 Need to be good readers. These parts could be further split if you want three or four Narrators.

Angels Again there's room for great flexibility here. As mentioned above, in the original production these were Brownies but they would also work well as a mixed all age group – plenty of scope for in-jokes as familiar church figures turn up as angels!

Christmas Crib Service and talk

Crib services are strange beasts. The example on pages 27–8 is how we do ours. It's hardly original, but this is not a time for the unusual – parents and children value the traditions of Christmas. We almost didn't put this in the book as what we have to offer is so orthodox, but Christmas wouldn't be complete without a crib service and perhaps this book is similar.

Because there is no separate talk in this service – the 'talk' runs throughout and is intertwined with the activity – we offer an outline service sheet below as an example of how the service works.

Don't be tempted to miss out taking the children for a walk round the church – this has many objectives, but the most important is that the children move at the point when they will be getting sore behinds!

You need:

✦ a crib scene – a large box, open at the front, with hay in it. If you can get your friendly neighbourhood DIY bod to decorate it so that it looks like a stable you're on to a winner!

✦ the various statues for the crib. If your church doesn't have these, various ecclesiastical suppliers sell them. They are not cheap, but they are an investment. Alternatively make your own in Sunday Club using varnished eggs for heads, cardboard tubes, scraps of material – you know the sort of thing!

✦ a candle in a portable stand – many churches refer to these as 'lights'.

✦ adults to supervise.

✦ a large area cleared at the front.

Publicize around the schools, health centres, toddler groups and expect a lot of children. Have tea, squash and Christmas cake for afterwards. You might like to ask children to come dressed for the Nativity as any appropriate character they like (if they all come as camels you'll have to improvise).

Talk to your local school and get copies of this year's carols. Learn them and include them. Chances are the children won't know some of the more 'churchy' carols. The BBC *Come and Praise* books are used in many primary schools and you may be able to borrow a set.

Service outline

Start with a good carol, then get out the statue of Mary. Ask the children who she is. If you live in a predominantly Christian part of the country, they may all know the story backwards, so expect plenty of reaction at this service! Who did Mary meet one day, quite unexpectedly and quite a shock? The angel, and what did the angel tell Mary? and so on.

Get as far as Mary being very pregnant, then ask all the children who have dressed for the roles mentioned so far to come out and form a tableau. Talk it through, and then sing another carol.

Continue with the story, with questions and answers as before. Get to the birth of Jesus in the stable, pop in the baby, and then get out the children in costume again. Sing another carol.

Prior to the service, you have positioned the shepherd statues at one side of the church – we put ours near the door. So when you get to the shepherds, take all the children for a walk to go and find them. Not too far – they were only just outside Bethlehem. Give the statues to some children to bring back. This may mean upping your insurance policy – but never mind, it's worth it!

All process back to the crib, ask the children to put in the shepherds – resist the temptation to tidy the scene up – and get out any children dressed as shepherds as you sing a shepherdy carol.

Then it's time for the Wise Men / Kings. Position these as far from the crib as you can, to stress the distance, and put the light nearby, to represent the star. Take the children down to get the statues once you've covered that part of the story, and light the candle. Give that to an older child, (and walk back with that child). Give out the Wise Men and then all process back to the crib. Put in the statues, bring out the relevantly dressed wise girls and boys, and sing a carol about the Kings.

Now it's time for some prayers. See the service outline for how we do ours – a series of responses, and the Lord's Prayer. The prayers must be brief and to the point – the children will be getting fidgety by now, despite two bursts of movement.

It's probably a good idea to sing 'Away in a manger' at the end, if only for all the parents and grandparents. This is the one traditional carol that most children sing with their parents.

And so to cake and drinks. Merry Christmas!

An example of a traditional Crib Service outline can be found on pages 27-8:

Sample choral prayers

We thank you God for Christmas time

Joy, joy to the world

For family fun at Christmas time

Joy, joy to the world

For singing and praising and gifts and all

Joy, joy to the world

For the light that was born on Christmas night

Joy, joy to the world

For Jesus, a baby, the Son of God

Joy, joy to the world

Joy, joy to the world

Joy, joy to the world.

Version worked out by the Sunday Club at St Peter's, Hemel Hempstead

We thank you God for today and every day

Joy, joy to the world

For books and toys and family and friends

Joy, joy to the world

For holidays and people who make them special

Joy, joy to the world

For sunshine and frost, rain and snow,

For all that makes the green earth grow.

For the light that was born on Christmas night

Joy, joy to the world

For Jesus, a baby, the Son of God

Joy, joy to the world

Joy, joy to the world

Joy, joy to the world.

Christmas rap

You've heard of the stable and the star
The famous Wise Men who travelled so far
You've heard of the shepherds and the angels' song
The cattle, the manger and all that went on.

Perhaps you know of the baby boy
That Herod the king tried to destroy
And Mary and Joseph in Bethlehem
The taxes, the census, the crowds and then,

It might be that you've wondered about
This tiny baby and you doubt
How any baby could matter to us
So much that people make all this fuss.

Messiah, Emmanuel, chosen one,
Jesus the King, God's own son,
Son of God yet born on earth
A baby counted of such great worth.

Why all the fuss, all the jamboree?
It's Christmas – what's that to you or me?
The whole thing starts with a baby's cry
Stop and think, ask yourself why.

Nativity play

Script

Organ	FANFARE
Messenger	(*Pops up from pulpit?, reads from scroll*)
	Hear ye, hear ye. Our most high, clever and all round excellent rulers announce their exciting new tax.
All	BOO, HISS
Messenger	All citizens are to report to the town of their birth for their chance to sign up and pay up. This means you! (*Points at Mary and Joseph*)
Mary	I can't travel in my condition.
Messenger	And it means now!
Narrator	So off they went on the long journey to Bethlehem.
Organ	MUSIC FOR JOURNEY SEQUENCE

(*About two minutes, evocative of plodding along hot, dusty road, with clear rhythm for Mary and Joseph to pick up in their movements.*)

Narrator	When they arrived . . .

(*Three Innkeepers enter and stand in different areas. Mary and Joseph go to each in turn.*)

Joseph	(*Knocks on first door. Innkeeper mimes opening door.*) Good evening, we were wondering if . . .

(*He tails off as the Innkeeper shakes his head.*)

Mary	(*Knocks on second door. Innkeeper opens door.*) We've just arrived from the country and were wondering if . . .

(*She tails off as the Innkeeper shakes her head.*)

Joseph	(*Knocks on third door. Innkeeper opens door.*) We're very tired and we just need a bed for the . . .

(*He tails off as the Innkeeper shakes his head.*)

(*Mary and Joseph begin to walk away. The Innkeeper calls them back.*)

Innkeeper	Wait a moment – if you really don't mind where you sleep, there's a bit of room in the stable if you don't mind sharing with Allan and Ronni our asses. (*Substitute names of clergy/wardens.*)
Narrator	So Mary and Joseph settled down for the night.

(There could be a choir/music group piece here. During this the shepherds and angel take up position.)

Narrator	So that night the baby was born and in a field not too far away . . .
Organ	FANFARE
Angel	I am the messenger of the Almighty God . . .
Shepherd 1	We will pay our tax, I promise . . .
Narrator	But the Angel brought them even better news so they set off to find the baby.
Organ	MUSIC FOR JOURNEY SEQUENCE

(About two minutes. Something rustic – 'Archers' style. Shepherds set off to music and then gather around Joseph and Mary with baby.)

Narrator	And in the East, a great new star appeared in the sky.
Star	I am the heavenly messenger of the Almighty God.
Wise Man	What is this shining star I see?
	Let us go on bended knee
	And follow it both here and there
	With precious gifts and offerings rare.
Narrator	They soon gave up the bended knee bit and travelled instead by camel.
Organ	MUSIC FOR JOURNEY SEQUENCE

(About two minutes, regal. Music brings the Wise Men to the scene. All now freeze in a tableau around Mary and Joseph.)

Organ	FANFARE
Messenger	Now look here, your rulers, the Romans . . .
Narrator	Rulers come and rulers go, but after today, the world will never be the same again. So . . .
Mary	Rejoice with me and greet my Son.
Narrator	And a merry Christmas . . .
All	To everyone.

Shepherds' play

Script

(The Shepherds enter, line up and with a 'one, two, three', or strokes on a tambourine, perform their Shepherds' Rap with simple movements:)

Shepherds

We're shepherds and we tend our sheep

With a hey no nonny nonny nay

All night long we hear their bleat

With a hey no, bah bah bah.

We're shepherds and we work all night

With a hey no nonny nonny nay

When you're asleep with lions we fight

With a hey no, roar roar roar.

We're shepherds and we're strong and tough

With a hey no nonny nonny nay –

Narrators 1 & 2   I think dear friends we've heard enough

All   With a nonny, nonny, nonny nonny, nonny nonny no.

Narrator 1   Listen.

Narrator 2   It's night time.

Narrator 1   Cold dark night

Narrator 2   Stars in the sky

Narrator 1   Bright, frost bright

Narrator 2   Shining clear in still, cold air.

Narrator 1   A special night?

Shepherd 1   Oh yes, a very special night indeed. We'll tell you all about it. Ready, Shepherds?

Shepherds   We're shepherds and we tend our sheep

With a hey no nonny nonny nay –

Narrator 2	No not that.
Old Shepherd	Nonny nonny no . . .
Cool Shepherd	Hey cool it Grandad.
Shepherd 2	But it's our party piece.
Narrator 2	Never mind that. Listen . . .
Narrator 1	Just beyond the sky
Narrator 2	Around the shining stars
Narrator 1	The angels are meeting . . .
Shepherds	Angels!
Old Shepherd	Angels!
Shepherds	Grandad!
Narrator 1	The angels are meeting.
Shepherd 3	Do you think they'd like to hear our party piece?
Narrator 1	Shepherds disappear, let the Angels draw near.
Shepherds	We're shepherds and we're told to go With a hey no nonny nonny nay But we'll be back before you know With a hey no, bye, bye, bye.

(*The shepherds move off and the angels enter talking.*)

Angel 1	Look, I should be the one to carry the message.
Angel 2	Well I'm the brightest.
Angel 3	So what, I've got all my badges: flying beginners, flying intermediate, flying expert, somersaults, backward flying, synchronized flying, materializing . . .
Angel 1	Humility?
Narrator 1	All right, all right, but . . .
Angels	What is the message?

Angel 3	You started it.
Angel 1	Did not.
Angel 3	Did.
Angel 1	Did not.
Angel 3	Did, did, did.
Narrator 1	All right, all right, but . . .
Angels	What is the message?
Angel 2	I'm the only one who can do it 'cos I've learnt the script.
Narrator 2	At last we're getting somewhere.
Angel 2	Listen: Greetings Earthlings, Stardate 00,00, our five year mission to spread new light . . .
Narrator 2	Wrong script!
Angel 1	Anyway, you can't do it, your wings are too scruffy – I bet you're still taking two bottles into the meteor shower.
Angel 2	The cheek of it! Me, I just wash and glow.
Narrator 1	All right, all right, but . . .
Angels	What is the message?
Angel 3	I know, why can't we wait 2000 years and e-mail it down?
Narrator 1	But this message can't wait.
Narrator 2	The news is urgent.
Narrator 1	A baby is on the way.
Narrator 2	There can be no delay.
Narrator 1	Clear heaven away – go on, shoo . . .

(*Angels reluctantly move to the back. Shepherds move forward.*)

Narrator 2	The earth is where this story turns.
Narrator 1	Listen.

Narrator 2	It's night time.
Narrator 1	Cold dark night
Narrator 2	Stars in the sky
Narrator 1	Bright, frost bright
Narrator 2	Shining clear in still, cold air.
Narrator 1	A special night?
Narrator 2	Shepherds are at work in the fields. Tending their sheep.
Shepherd 1	Shh. All of you, be quiet, I can hear something.

(*Angels argue off: 'I want to do it,' 'No let me,' etc.*)

Shepherd 2	Voices.
Shepherd 1	Heavenly voices.
Shepherd 3	But what are they saying?
Angel 4	I'll do it. (*To narrator*) Here, give me that message.

(*Narrator hands over scroll. Angel 4 marches boldly up to the Shepherds who cower in fear.*)

	Don't be afraid. I bring good news which will bring joy to all people.
Narrator 1	And this is what the angel told them:
Angel 4	This very day in David's town your Saviour is born. Go, you will find a baby wrapped in cloth and lying in a manger.
Narrators & Shepherds	A Saviour? A baby? In a manger?
Narrator 2	But before they could take it in, all the other angels burst out of heaven desperate to get in on the act.

(*Angels run on.*)

Narrator 1	And they couldn't believe the news either.
Angels	A Saviour? A baby? In a manger?
Narrator 2	They were so excited, they couldn't contain themselves.
Angels	Yeah, whoopee, hooray (*etc.*)

Narrator 1	Or if you prefer:
Angels	Glory to God and peace on earth.
Narrator 2	Overcoming their fear, the shepherds set off at once.
Old Shepherd	I can't go all that way at my age.
Cool Shepherd	If you wanna see the show, you just gotta go.
Shepherds	Come on Grandad.
Narrator 2	And they found the baby just as they had been told, lying in a crib, in a manger.

(Shepherds move to gather round crib.)

Narrator 1	Listen.
Narrator 2	It's night time.
Narrator 1	Cold dark night
Narrator 2	Stars in the sky
Narrator 1	Bright, frost bright
Narrator 2	Shining clear in still, cold air.
Narrator 1	A special night?
Shepherd 1	Oh yes, a very special night.
Angels	Glory to God and peace on earth.
Shepherd 1	And so say all of us,
All	With a nonny, nonny, nonny, nonny, nonny, nonny YES!

Crib Service

We welcome you to this special service. Please feel free to sit on the kneelers at the front if you would like to, or in the pews if you feel more comfortable there.

The crib story: Mary and Joseph.

Song: **Little donkey**

The crib story: Jesus is born.

Song: **Infant Holy**

The crib story: The shepherds.

For this part of the story we will be moving to the back of the church: please hang on to your child!

Song: **It was on a starry night**

The crib story: The Wise Men.

Once again, we are on the move around the church!

Song: **O little town of Bethlehem**

Prayers

Leader   Jesus was born in Bethlehem.

All   **Thank you God.**

           Jesus had a mother and family too.

All   **Thank you God.**

           Jesus came because God loves us.

All   **Thank you God.**

           Jesus loves each one of us.

All   **Thank you God.**

           We can love each other too.

All   **Thank you God.**

           The angels sang when the baby was born.

All   **We sing too.**

           The shepherds came when the baby was born.

All   **We came too.**

           The Kings found the stable where the baby was born.

All   **We have found it too.**

           We come to praise God.

All	**We come to praise God too.**
	Glory to God in the highest.
All	**And peace to all people on earth.**
	Our Father, who art in heaven,
	hallowed be thy name;
	thy kingdom come;
	thy will be done;
	on earth as it is in heaven.
	Give us this day our daily bread.
	And forgive us our trespasses,
	As we forgive those who trespass against us.
	And lead us not into temptation;
	but deliver us from evil.
	For thine is the kingdom, the power, and the glory,
	for ever and ever. Amen.
Song:	**Away in a manger**
	'The Glory of the Lord shall be revealed and all people shall see it.' (Isaiah 40.5)
Leader	As we go out into the Christmas night,
All	**Come with us, Lord.**
Leader	As we lie down to sleep on Christmas night,
All	**Be with us, Lord.**
Leader	As we wake to the light of Christ,
All	**Come into us, Lord. Amen.**

The Blessing

Epiphany

The Tale of the Wise Ones

Introduction

The script for this play can be found on pages 32–6. The play takes as its starting point the fact that we know little about these characters from the Bible, but they pose profound questions about the infant they visit. It is suitable for Christmas or Epiphany.

The play was first performed at St Peter's Church, St Albans, Christmas 1994 by the Sunday School and Brownies, with an age range of 5–11. As the production notes below make clear, it is flexible in cast size and age range and would work well with some teenagers or adults in the cast. There is also the possibility of expanding the play as suggested.

Characters

Wise Ones   The play needs a minimum of four Wise Ones. They can be any age, but since the roles are simple, mostly processing with a few spoken lines, they would suit young children, or they could form a mix of all-ages. They can be male or female and a joke is made of this at the start of the play.

Narrator   The Narrator has most of the words and so needs to be a competent speaker. The words could be read from the pulpit/lectern to minimize the amount of learning involved – they could be read from a scroll or large book. The Narrator could be an older child, teenager or adult or could be split between various people to increase the number of roles and variety of voices.

Star   This is best suited to a younger child. The role has lots of movement and a simple poem.

Chief Villager   In many ways this is a second Narrator role. It could be read from the opposite side of the acting area, but would be better if learnt so that the Chief Villager could move around amongst the action. The part would suit an older child, teenager or adult.

Villagers   These have lots of mime and one-word responses. In the original production the Villagers and Chief Villager were Brownies since these could be rehearsed separately in their own sessions, coming together with the rest of the cast at the dress rehearsal.

Herod   Herod has a simple poem. He can be attended by very young children as his Pages.

Costume

This play would work well with traditional head-dresses, crowns, peasant dress, etc. Or you can be more imaginative, dressing the Wise Ones in flamboyant modern dress, the Star as a rock legend, the villagers in 'yokel' costume and so on. The important thing is to make the stage look bright and interesting with as much colour as possible.

Music

Music plays a big part in this play. There are the Three Blind Mice songs (see text on p. 37), the journey music, Herod's fanfare and the processional hymn at the end. This is a good opportunity to involve choirs, music groups, the organist, the folk group or whoever is available. In a church where the choir usually sing an anthem, this could be placed in the middle of the play, perhaps during one of the journey sections. This will expand the range and number of people involved in the production and, since music is an important part of most worship, will help to integrate the play into the service.

If a large group of musicians is unavailable, you could use a recorder for the songs and pre-recorded music for the journey.

One way of involving the congregation, in addition to the procession at the end, is to photocopy the songsheet on page 37 and encourage everyone to join in with the songs at the appropriate times.

Expanding the play

In addition to the music mentioned above, the play could be expanded with:

- ✦ a simple dance sequence for the journey showing growing tiredness, heavy walking through the sand, a sand storm etc.;

- ✦ a dance sequence for the Villagers' work with repetitive patterns and small group sequences of, for example, washing clothes, felling trees, hunting, cooking;

- ✦ an improvised scene at Herod's court, with an elaborate ritual of bowing and presenting arms before the King, intended to increase the sense of pomp and importance.

After the play, there is a processional hymn in which the congregation follow the Wise Ones and Star into the stable. You could form a simple arch with bodies through which everyone has to pass before walking around the church as they sing and go back to their seats. This can then be followed with a short talk picking up on the questions at the end of the play.

The Tale of the Wise Ones

Script

(The full cast are gathered around the acting area to sing the opening song (see full text on p. 37). As they sing, the Wise Ones move into position ready to turn around or pop up as they each speak their first line.)

All	*(To the tune of Three Blind Mice)* Three Wise Men, Three Wise Men, See where they go, See where they go, They all go after a star one night Led on the way by its shining light, When the star stops they see such a sight, Those three Wise Men.
One	One
Two	Two
Three	Three
Narrator	The story of the three Wise Men . . .
Four	Four!
Narrator	*(Annoyed)* Four Wise Men.

(Wise Ones cough loudly. More Wise Ones can join at this point.)

Narrator	All right, have it your own way, Wise Men, Women and Children. Okay? Happy now? No more Wise Ones hidden anywhere?

(Wise Ones shake their heads.)

	Not hidden under the pews? No Wise Ones disguised as clergy? No, silly idea. Right. On with the show. Quickly before anyone else pops up. Star, you're on.
Star	I am a star shining bright, Leading the Wise Ones through the night. Come on you lot, don't be slow, Pack your camels, it's time to go.

(Music to accompany packing camels and journey. The Wise Ones and Star set off around the church or space, leaving the acting area free. During the following narration, the Villagers assemble. They mime various jobs, sowing seed, cooking etc.)

Narrator   At last everything's packed and they set off and you know what it's like, no sooner are you going than someone needs to stop. Eventually, tired, hungry and thirsty they see a village on the horizon.

Chief Villager   Villagers of Anyville, listen to me.

Villagers   We're listening.

Chief Villager   Strangers, I see strangers on the horizon.

Villagers   Oh.

(They go back to work. Pause.)

Chief Villager   Villagers of Anyville, listen to me.

Villagers   We're listening.

Chief Villager   The strangers, they're getting nearer.

Villagers   Oh.

(They go back to work. Pause.)

Chief Villager   Villagers of Anyville, listen to me.

Villagers   We're listening.

Chief Villager   They're here, the strangers. They're here.

Villagers   Oh.

(They go back to work. Pause.)

Chief Villager   Don't you want to hear what they have to say?

Villagers   No.

(They go back to work. Pause.)

Chief Villager   Well I do. Welcome strangers. Who are you, and where are you going?

Wise Ones   We're Wise Folk.

Chief Villager   Oh modest!

Wise Ones   We're following a star.

Chief Villager	And stupid. Where's the star leading you?
Wise Ones	We don't know.
Chief Villager	So that's what it takes to be a Wise Person, I must remember that next time I sit an exam. I suppose you want food and water?
Narrator	Now *you're* getting wise.
Chief Villager	Villagers of Anyville, listen to me.
Villagers	We're listening.
Chief Villager	The strangers here want food and water. Shall we give it to them?

(*Villagers get in a huddle and mumble. Then Villager 1 stands up and speaks.*)

Villager 1	One simple question O Wise Ones: what's in it for us?

(*Wise Ones get in a huddle and mumble.*)

Narrator	That's the trouble with Wise Folk, ask a simple question and you get a three-hour lecture, two days of discussion, a thorough and detailed Royal Commission and at the end of it . . .
One	Well, it just seems like the right thing to do.
Chief Villager	Villagers of Anyville, listen to me.
Villagers	We're listening.
Chief Villager	There's a simple choice here, do we help these strangers or not?
Villagers	(*Individually*) We're too busy.
	No time.
	We haven't enough food.
	They might drink the stream dry.
Narrator	In other words –
Villagers	On your camel.
All	Those Wise Folk,
	Those Wise Folk,
	Onward they go,
	Onward they go,
	They ask for help but try as they might

No one will offer a bed for the night,

Weary, they follow the star's bright light,

Those tired Wise Folk.

(*During the above the Villagers clear the stage and the Wise Ones and Star continue their journey.*)

Narrator   Then King Herod gets to hear of the journey.

(*Fanfare. Herod enters with great pomp. He could be accompanied by lackeys.*)

Herod   If you Wise Ones find a king

Hurry back to tell me.

I would like to welcome him,

Now quickly on your journey.

(*Music. Herod exits, more journey.*)

Narrator   At last their journey seems to be at an end. The star stops. And – they find themselves at –

Wise Ones   A stable!

Narrator   Yes, they've come all this way for –

Wise Ones   A stable!

One   We came to worship

Two   To adore

Three   To find a palace

Four   Not a stable door.

One   We're clever.

Two   Rich.

Three   Powerful.

Wise Ones   We're not going in there!

Narrator   Well, there our story must end. The Wise Ones are too proud to go where the Star has led them. So that's it, finito, game over, time to pack up and go home. Unless . . .

They hear a sound from inside the stable. An ordinary, everyday sound. Amidst the cattle and the straw, a baby cries.

What should they do?

	Should they go in?
	Should they report at once to King Herod?
	Have they really come all this way, for a baby in a stable?
All	Those Wise Folk,
	Those Wise Folk,
	What should they do,
	What should they do?
	Pack up now and go back home?
	Saddle their camels and continue to roam?
	Or enter and see if a King is at home?
	Those muddled Wise Folk.
Narrator	Decisions, decisions. A story of decisions.
	Should the Villagers have fed the strangers?
	Should the Wise Ones return to King Herod?
	What's so special about this baby anyway?
	Perhaps they'll never know, unless . . .
One	I'm going in.
Two	Me too.
Three	And me.
Four	And me.
Narrator	And . . . you?

(*Processional hymn. All follow the Wise Ones.*)

36

The Tale of the Wise Ones

Songsheet

To the tune of Three Blind Mice.

Three Wise Men,

Three Wise Men,

See where they go,

See where they go.

They all go after a star one night,

Led on the way by its shining light,

When the star stops they see such a sight,

Those three Wise Men.

Those Wise Folk,

Those Wise Folk,

Onward they go,

Onward they go,

They ask for help but try as they might

No one will offer a bed for the night,

Weary, they follow the star's bright light,

Those tired Wise Folk.

Those Wise Folk,

Those Wise Folk,

What should they do,

What should they do?

Pack up now and go back home?

Saddle their camels and continue to roam?

Or enter and see if a King is at home?

Those muddled Wise Folk.

Candlemas

Candlemas Service and talk

This is the first Sunday in February (the feast day is 2 February) and is becoming rapidly more widely 'done' by all varieties of church. The festival is to mark the time when Joseph and Mary took the baby Jesus to the Temple, as told in Luke 2.22–40. *The Promise of his Glory* (CHP/Mowbray 1991) has some super services for adults, so here's an outline for all-age worship.

If you want to use this service as a real point of outreach, invite back all the people/children who have been baptized in the last year, making sure you have refreshments afterwards – we've had a terrific turnout the times that we tried this, and it was a great way to remake the contact with those families.

Beforehand

You need:

✦ A4 sheets with an outline picture of a burning candle. See photocopy master on page 106 or better still draw your own.

✦ A large (e.g. 2m) picture of a candle, similar design to the A4, but hopefully coloured, and stuck on to an appropriate place in the church. Our design scaled up would be ideal as it's simple and clear.

✦ Every child (and adults if they want) needs access to some colouring implements.

✦ Everyone needs a candle (6in is adequate. If you have the wax catchers so much the better).

✦ Tapers.

Hymns/songs include:

Morning has broken, God is love, Every star shall sing a carol,
Hail to the Lord's anointed.

Collects:

POG p. 359 No. 85; p. 357 No. 78; ASB p. 450 year 2.

Talk outline

Luke 2.22–40

The Bible reading would be best read as a dramatized piece, with a narrator for each paragraph, someone to read the quotes from Jewish law (as in verses 23 and 24), and Simeon. If Simeon can be an old man with a beard, so much the better! You may wish to edit the reading down, to exclude some of the details that will confuse children and are not vital to the story.

Get the children up near to you first if you can. A square of carpet is a good investment! Ask them to listen to the reading carefully as they will need to know the story so they can join in later.

After the reading talk about baptism, ask the children how old most children are when they come to be baptized. If you have a baptism at this service, ask the parents if you can borrow the child, and talk about the age at which most children are baptized in the Anglican Church. Why do we bring children to be baptized? Do you think it's a good idea to celebrate the birth of a child in church?

Then tell the children that what happened to Jesus in the story wasn't the same as baptism, but that the idea behind it is very similar. We bring children to baptism to thank God for them, and that's what Mary and Joseph were doing.

Run through the bare bones of the story in question and answer form. You may wish to have a simple quiz: one side of the children against another side, or children v. adults with appropriate weighting for children (you could slip in some 'children's culture' references such as questions about pop stars to even things up!). The kind of questions to ask are:

> What were Jesus' parents called?
>
> Where did they take him?
>
> What was the name of the old man?
>
> What was the name of the old woman?
>
> Can you remember anything that Simeon said to Mary?
>
> Does anyone know what we call the piece of poetry that Simeon spoke?
>
> and so on.

If you're running it as a quiz, it's good fun to make up some simple rules – hands up to answer, I'll count to five and you have to put your hand up during that time, and so on. You can have an older child as scorer and, again, you can weight the scores in the younger children's favour.

Another way of running a quiz with a complicated reading such as this (it contains strange names and is not particularly well known) is to organize teams and give them a large printout of the reading, so that the task becomes as much research as recall.

Before moving from this section into the talk, it may help to re-run the reading at this point, to reinforce the story.

Then point out that today we remember our baptism, and we thank God for it, and repeat the promises that were made for us at baptism, and so remind ourselves of becoming members of the church.

Extension and alternatives (perhaps for older children) are to ask:

> What do we want for our children?
>
> What are our hopes and fears?
>
> What would the children like to see happen during their lives?

Aim to talk for no more than ten minutes.

Prayers

Use the candle pictures.

Older children and adults: in your candle, write/draw pictures of the people that are special to you and that you would like to pray for.

Younger children: colour in the candle.

The organist/music group play suitable music whilst the activity goes on.

Everyone processes with their picture to the large candle, where a couple of people Blu-tack the smaller pictures around the larger candle.

If you have a choir and are of that tradition, sing the Nunc Dimittis.

We then use the central portion of the Baptism Service as a renewal of vows; We recommend section 46 (ASB, p. 244), then 47, 48, 53, 54. (Words may need to be carefully rewritten in the introductory sections.)

After this, sing a suitable song, and then distribute the candles to everyone (including the children). Using the words from section 57, we then pass the light around the church. Keeping the candles alight, all say the prayer at 61 together. Children know that candles are dangerous, and it's quite magical to see them at this point. We do recommend the judicious placing of extra water in buckets, and fire extinguishers, though!

We finish by singing a song, and the blessing.

Mothering Sunday and Families

Family tree prayers and talk

Introduction

These prayers take the form of simple family trees, which are drawn and offered to God as a way of praying for families.

Age range:	All age.
Materials:	Paper and pencils/pens – enough for every family grouping in church.
	Something to lean on whilst drawing would also be useful.
	The leader will need a flip chart, large sheet of paper or an OHP.
Working space:	In church.

Method

You will need to have prepared, either on a flip chart or an overhead projector, your own family tree, going back to your grandparents.

Also prepare Jesus' family tree. (Mary's parents are believed to have been called Anna and Joachim. We don't have any names for Joseph's parents.)

Assemble the children in their listening place. Show them your family tree and ask if anyone knows what this strange diagram is?

Talk them though how it works, who the various names are, especially if some of them are present. Be particularly sensitive to those for whom talk of family might be distressing – children who have just lost a grandparent or children who have only one parent living at home.

Then take them through the family tree for Jesus.

Send the children back to their families, to draw a family tree for each family present. Single people can also do this – it is important that everyone in church joins in drawing a family tree.

It may be helpful to get your music people to play some gentle music if your congregation are happier without being able to hear the buzz.

Note: Again there is a need for sensitivity here because of remarriages, single parent families and the uncertainties which children can face, and it may be that this section is inappropriate because it focuses too strongly on the family structure, rather than family love. Alternatives would be to write or draw prayers for our families, or for younger children to draw themselves with their family.

When the trees or other offerings are drawn – and it takes quite a few minutes – ask them to pass them to the end of the rows/pews. Stewards then gather them as an offertory, and they are placed on the altar/table. Introduce the idea of God's family tree – which includes everyone. You can connect this with the reason that we pray for the Church and for the World.

A prayer is said asking God to bless all the families represented. The Collect for year 1, Christmas 2 in the ASB is as follows;

> Heavenly Father,
> whose blessed Son shared at Nazareth
> the life of an earthly home,
> help us to live as the holy family,
> united in love and obedience,
> and bring us at last to our home in heaven;
> through Jesus Christ our Lord.

Or devise a prayer such as:

> Thank you God for families,
> For members of our family that we see every day
> And those we see less often.
> In a moment of silence, say your own quiet prayer for your own family . . .
>
> Thank you for the family of the church – our special Christian friends –
> Both here in . . . and all over the world.
> Thank you for your big family,
> The family of all men, women and children.
>
> Help us to love our close family,
> Our wider family,
> Our church family,
> And everyone.
> Amen.

Family song

The words of this song can be found on page 47. Sing the song to the tune of One, two, three, four, five, Once I caught a fish alive. Although children and adults will be familiar with the tune, it is quite fast and requires concentration. It's ideal for having fun with in church as everyone learns the song together. Once the congregation is reasonably proficient, try splitting it into different parts.

Family rap

Introduction

Like all the raps in this book, the one on page 48 can be rehearsed by children in their own session and then presented to the whole church when everyone joins together. It can also be used as a basis for children writing their own raps. Aim for a sharp, clear delivery. To maintain interest, if you have a large enough group, you could split the verses between smaller groups. You could also use a rhythm backing from a tape or keyboard.

Age range:	7–12. The age range will depend on how the idea is developed; teenagers might like to perform their own raps with accompaniment.
Working space:	Space in which to prepare away from the main church – could be quite noisy!

Family drama and talk

The simple drama on page 49 and the talk will need some preparation beforehand. The drama is designed to involve all-ages. Group 3 has mostly simple improvised drama, whilst the other two have various simple lines. These could be spoken by the whole group together or split between group members as appropriate.

Start with the drama and follow this with the talk. It would be possible to put a hymn in between – thus the optional last line of the drama.

Drama

Three different groups are spread around the church. Group 3 have actions to perform so need to be where they can be seen. It will be most effective if the other two groups are concealed amongst the congregation and simply stand at the right moment – taking everyone by surprise.

Talk

The talk is presented as a series of bullet points to be developed and elaborated to suit your own style and approach. There are also two pew sheets which cover these areas (see pages 111–12).

✦ Talk about the drama and ask for comments – did anyone recognize their own family?

✦ Ask the congregation to brainstorm families in the Bible – how many can they think of? There is an option here of asking the congregation to search their Bibles to find families – write these on a flip chart or OHP.

✦ How can family members help each other – on special occasions? – when things go wrong? – every day? Relate the answers to the Bible references if appropriate.

✦ What does 'the family of God' mean?

✦ Ask again, 'So why did God create families?'

Family song

To the tune of One, two, three, four, five, Once I caught a fish alive.

One, two, three, four, five,

Families can be any size.

Six, seven, eight, nine, ten,

Girls and boys and women and men.

Uncles, aunts and cousins too,

Lots of people to help you.

The church is one big family,

With God at the top of the family tree.

Family rap

Far from home
In a stable born
A baby cries
In the early morn.

Family life
Family life
Family, family life.

Age of twelve
Lost one day.
When he's found
He's heard to say,

Who are my brothers?
My sisters too?
He meant everyone
Both me and you.

Family life
Family life
Family, family life.

The day he died
Was hung up high,
He thought of others
As his mother cried.

But there's more news
Of which we sing.
Death's not the end
He came to bring,

Family life
Family life
Family, family life.

Family drama

Group 1	Why did God create families?
Group 2	So they could enjoy life in harmony – like this:
Group 3	(*Improvised peaceful family – eating and drinking together harmoniously perhaps?*)
Group 1	Stop.

(*Group 3 immediately stop and freeze.*)

Group 2	So they could be nice to each other like this:
Group 3	(*Improvised friendly greetings, 'hi', 'hello', back-slapping, handshakes etc.*)
Group 1	Stop.

(*Group 3 immediately stop and freeze.*)

Group 2	So they could play games and sport together.
Group 3	(*Improvised mime of games such as football, table tennis*)
Group 1	Stop!

(*Group 3 immediately stop and freeze.*)

Group 3	GET REAL!
All	All very tidy, oh so neat
Group 2	My family rushes me off my feet
All	Family life can drive you crazy
Group 1	My family are all too lazy
Group 2	My family won't eat their peas
All	So why did God create families?
Optional:	
Group 1	We'll find out after this short break.

Lent and Easter

Suffering: service and talk

The Third Sunday in Lent in the ASB has the theme of 'The King and the Kingdom: Suffering'. If your family service falls on that day you may well be thinking about alternatives, but here is an outline of a service that we conducted at St Alban's Church, Hemel Hempstead.

Hymns:

There are more than you would think! Trust and obey, What a friend we have in Jesus, When I needed a neighbour, He who would valiant be, Lord of all hopefulness, Lead us heavenly Father, Guide me O thou great redeemer, A man there lived in Galilee, Father hear the prayer we offer, Be bold, be strong, Be thou my vision, etc. 'My God is so big' crops up as part of the talk.

Start with an appropriate **greeting**; *Patterns for Worship* or *The Pattern of our Days* are helpful here.

Hymn 1: something to get the people gathered and into the right frame of mind.

Collect for the day, followed by the **Lord's Prayer**. We love the sung version (music in *Come and Praise*) and it lifts what can be a very adult part of the worship.

Hymn 2 here, or sung version of the Lord's Prayer.

Reading: 2 Kings 5.1–14 – the healing of Naaman. Gather the children at the front. You must have a good reader, who addresses the foregathered children, as the story is quite long, and has many threads running through it. There are also quite a few comic moments – as when the King of Israel panics at Naaman's arrival – and it's a shame to lose them. You could try rewriting the story, or rehearsing a dramatized reading with exaggerated voices for the different characters.

Go through the story with the children, either as a question and answer session, or in the form of a quiz. For ideas about organizing quizzes see page 40 (Candlemas section). Don't expect them to have heard it too clearly, and go over the details – that Naaman is a 'baddy', and what wars were like – gory! What being taken as a slave meant for the little girl, what leprosy is like. (Remind them of a recent 'Blue Peter' appeal?)

Then act out the story, but not with specific children portraying individual characters: they all play everyone, all the way through, and what they are really portraying is the emotion of the story.

Use a still picture format to keep the results simple, clear and effective. You can join in to give children an idea of the kind of things they can do.

The scenes we used were:

Naaman in battle

— still pictures of fighting (arm raised as if throwing a spear?)

Naaman has leprosy

— a shocked expression with arms raised in disbelief

The slave girl being taken

— the instant of being captured

The girl speaks to Naaman's wife

— hand cupped to mouth

Packing the camels in readiness for the trip to Israel

— lifting heavy possessions on to camel's back

The King panicking

— caught in agitated midstride

Naaman is told to bathe in the Jordan

— hesitating on edge of water

Naaman is healed.

— arms raised in praise.

The above are all intended to be quick pictures with each child making their own version. You could spend more time and use several children in each picture, moulding them one by one into position. However, we favour the more instant version as it keeps things moving, allows everyone to participate at their own level and is a lot of fun!

Then draw the children together and ask how we can help others who are suffering – we talked about Bring and Buy sales, Comic Relief, Lent lunches, remembering others in our prayers, etc. Introduce the idea that a lot of suffering could be alleviated if we do something ourselves, even if it is in a small way. 'Small change – big difference' was a recent Comic Relief slogan and it's true.

Finish this section by singing the action song 'My God is so big'. We had taught this to our toddler group over the preceding weeks, so the tinies taught it to the grown-ups, and it was very successful.

Prayers: We had asked our Sunday Club children to write and read their own prayers, and we had pieces of card with the following areas written on, that the tinies held up during the prayers: sick people, homelessness, poor people, lonely people, pain, etc. Here is an example of a nine-year-old's prayer:

Pain and suffering

> Dear Lord,
> Pain is horrible, suffering is worse,
> from refugees to soldiers, tears to death,
> the world is full of it,
> but we could make hope,
> and we will.
> Amen.
>
> *Jim Lamont 1997*

We wish we could write them like that.

After the prayers, another **hymn.**

Find some **responses** to end with, to really collect the congregation together. We used some from the Iona Community Worship books (Wild Goose publications, 1988–91) – choose those that have a positive message about the work of God's Spirit in a hurting world.

Blessing

Final hymn

Penitence: dramatized prayer

These dramatic prayers of penitence were devised at a forty-minute workshop before the Ascension Day service at St Mary's Church, Hemel Hempstead, in 1997. They were then performed at the appropriate point in the service – outside the west door. They are suitable for interior or exterior use, but good sight lines are important. There were about twenty participants of all-ages from lower primary to upper elderly in our version, but the piece is very flexible and would work with four or five individuals or large numbers. They are simple in format, with no script to learn – although there are some improvised words.

Workshop session

Begin the session with a warm-up game. If the group are new to working with each other, we recommend 'Handshakers', played as follows:

Allow one minute (shorter with a small group), for everyone to move quickly around the room shaking hands with as many people as possible. As they shake they greet each other and tell each other their names. For example: 'Hello I'm Gordon', 'Hello Gordon, I'm Ronni', 'Goodbye Gordon', 'Goodbye Ronni'.

When you call time, see who can remember the most names and recite them. Repeat a few times so people get to know names.

A variant and development of this is 'Name Swappers'. In this version, as people greet each other, they take the name of the person they greet and retain it until they greet someone else. They then adopt this new name and so on. There is no time limit as people drop out when they can't remember who they are!

Devising the drama

After the game(s), move on to devising the actual drama.

The participants work in small groups of between two and five. Their task is to create a single move and phrase which expresses how we all try to avoid taking responsibility when things go wrong. Examples are:

The group turn and shrug shoulders, all saying, 'I didn't know, did I?'

or

The group turn and point at each other, shouting, 'She did it!'

or

The group turn and fold arms, saying, 'It's nothing to do with me.'

They are aiming for a tiny snippet of drama where they all move together, starting with backs to the congregation and turning to take up a pose and all speak their line in chorus. Stress the need for:

- ✦ someone to lead – giving a signal when the group is to turn;
- ✦ a short, clear, easily remembered phrase which expresses avoiding responsibility for actions;
- ✦ loud delivery;
- ✦ a clear gesture.

Allow the groups time to rehearse, then see each in turn. Encourage everyone to make sensitive comments and suggestions for improving the pieces.

Organize the groups into a semicircle in the space, starting with their backs to the congregation. Give them an order in which to perform and practise this a few times so that each group follows from the previous one.

You will end up with still pictures (tableaux) representing the moods and actions of the piece so far.

The next stage is to add some simple movement to represent how these attitudes and actions entangle us. One by one group members walk from their position to create a group body sculpture in the centre of the space. Aim for something spiky, irregular, twisted – a crown of thorns is a good image. The bodies intertwine to create this ugly, inharmonious image.

In our version this was done in silence and was very effective after the shouted words above. You could add music and develop this into more of a dance; or use appropriate words from a prayer of penitence, although this will take the edge off the next step.

The sculpture is held still and then a reader calls out short words or phrases from the Prayer of Absolution – which is to follow the drama. For example:

> *power*
>
> *love*
>
> *heal*
>
> *strengthen*
>
> *new life.*

As the words are spoken the sculpture unwinds and relaxes until the participants form a circle. They turn outwards, join hands and lift arms in praise before walking out to join the congregation.

Follow with the Prayer of Absolution:

> God who is both power and love,
> forgive *you* and free *you* from *your* sins,
> heal and strengthen *you* by his Spirit,
> and raise *you* to new life in Christ our Lord. **Amen**.

© Scottish Episcopal Church
Patterns for Worship (Church House Publishing, 1995), p. 50

Easter tableaux

Introduction

This idea is for Sunday Club or Junior Church to work on separately from the rest of the congregation; they then present it to the church. It can also work well as part of a Good Friday workshop. It is a simple, short set of tableaux (still pictures) with a strong impact based on the Easter message. It was first performed at a Good Friday workshop at St Peter's Church, St Albans, with an age range from six to fourteen.

Age range:	The idea requires an adult to work on the tableaux with the children and a confident young reader or adult to narrate the performance. The age of the children can be quite wide since tableaux can vary in sophistication and still be effective.
Working space:	Enough room for drama with the children/young people. Performance space – with as good a view as possible for the congregation.

Preparing the tableaux

Tips for tableaux

◆ Encourage simple, clear ideas.

◆ Rehearse so that everyone is sure of their place in each picture.

◆ Encourage the performers to 'snap' into each picture in unison, then hold it really still.

◆ Aim for a smooth transition from picture to picture.

◆ Look for variation as you move from picture to picture.

◆ Encourage different heights within pictures.

◆ Allow just long enough for those watching to get a good look at the pictures before moving on.

◆ Try working in mixed age groups – the older children can support the younger.

Working individually or in small groups, the children and young people create simple still pictures for each of the following titles (see text on p. 63).

JESUS WAS . . .

BORN	Example – picture of adult holding a baby
A CHILD	Example – playing with friends – circle game
A CARPENTER	Example – sawing, hammering
A TEACHER	Example – in full flow, talking to a crowd
A HEALER	Example – someone is about to jump for joy
A MIRACLE WORKER	Example – people point and look amazed
BETRAYED	Example – everyone points in the same direction (as if betraying Jesus)
CRUCIFIED	Example – all cover their heads as if heartbroken

This is followed by everyone shouting and clapping these last words:

DEAD (clap, clap, clap)

FINISHED (clap, clap, clap)

OVER (clap, clap, clap)

GONE FOR GOOD . . . (clap, clap, clap, CLAP)

All turn to leave, then when they reach the back of the performance area, turn as one, point to the congregation and say:

THAT'S WHAT YOU THINK!

Easter drama

Introduction

This is an ambitious drama requiring rehearsal beforehand, to be presented at a service or special event over the Easter period. It requires thoughtful stage management and direction but most of the individual parts are small, and many can be read from a script. Clear voices and a good pace are the most important dramatic elements. There are Bible readings and a congregational song included in the drama. It would be a simple matter to add congregational hymns at the start and end, and to finish with prayers or meditation to create a dramatic liturgy for all. See pages 64–7 for the full script.

Age range:	This is probably best suited to older children, teenagers and adults, since the lyrical nature and concepts involved make it less appropriate for the youngest children.
Working space:	Performance space – with as good a view as possible for the congregation.

Characters

The Chorus	Can be a mixture of ages. Younger children can be paired with someone older, and the parts can easily be split between more actors or combined if necessary.
Mary	This works well if played by an older child or teenager. Needs plenty of energy and life.
Angel	Can be either sex and any age with a good clear voice. It would be good if the Angel who speaks is also in the dance.
Disciples	These can double up with the chorus, or be a separate group.
Thomas	Probably best suited to an older man.
Dancers	These could be a mixture of age groups. See notes below.

Angel Dance

The story focus of this dance is Mary meeting the angels. The dance could take many forms and approaches according to the skills and style of the participants. It is probably best to have one person responsible for planning the outline of the dance and running the rehearsal sessions. If no one is available to take on this role, there is also the option of asking a local primary or secondary school to produce the dance for you. Dance is part of the National Curriculum for England and Wales and is even more prominent in the Scottish Curriculum. This might provide a good, 'real performance' focus for the school and be a useful link for the church.

Dance styles

The angels could be represented with a simple circle dance, suggesting symmetry of movement in contrast to the words that have gone before.

The Angel Dance could tell the story of Mary arriving at the tomb and the angels appearing and sending her away. This dance drama version could include people representing the tomb entrance who then turn into the angels.

A more radical suggestion is to use strong angular movements to create an abstract Angel Dance which is strongly representative of the other-worldliness, the strangeness of these events.

Music

Here there are many options. A simple chorus or hymn might be appropriate for the circle dance approach, and this may lend itself to the audience or congregation joining in the singing and, perhaps, the dancing.

An alternative for the circle dance would be to use traditional folk dance music, perhaps played live.

The other dance styles will need music that's appropriate and to your own tastes. We have rather odd tastes in this department and like to use music that people wouldn't expect: 'I want to know what love is', by Foreigner, would be a powerful contender here. A classical piece could be taken from the *Florida Suite* by Delius, with its lyrical opening redolent of the early morning. In the end all we can say is, go with what inspires you.

Easter rap

Introduction

Like all the raps in this book, the example on page 68 can be rehearsed by children in their own session and then presented to the whole church when everyone joins together. It can also be used as a basis for children writing their own raps. Aim for a sharp, clear delivery. To maintain interest, if you have a large enough group, you could split the verses between smaller groups. You could also use a rhythm backing from a tape or keyboard.

Age range:	7–12. The age range will depend on how the idea is developed; teenagers might like to perform their own raps with accompaniment.
Working space:	Space in which to prepare away from the main church – could be quite noisy!

Easter talk

A version of a traditional children's talk around an Easter garden.

You need a basic Easter garden with statues for this talk. The idea is to use the statues as a focus for talking about the resurrection and the impact it had on those who experienced it.

You could make the garden with the children at Good Friday workshops or they could work on it in Sunday Club in the weeks leading up to Easter.

John 20. 1–18

Gather the children. Read the account – perhaps splitting it between a number of voices placed strategically around the building. Alternatively, the magazine *Together with Children* featured 'The Boy who saw Easter' by Sheila Forsdyke in its March/April 1996 edition. This makes a lovely change from reading from the Gospel account – it's Easter through a child's eyes.

The boy who saw Easter

Matthew was sleeping soundly when the pet lamb by his side woke him.

'Baaa' it bleated, nuzzling his neck.

Ssh! Don't wake the others,' whispered Matthew, yawning and throwing off his goatskin blanket at the same time.

Inside the small, one-roomed house, his father, mother and younger sister were lying asleep under their goatskins. They did not stir. Matthew got up, splashed water from the stone water jar on to his face and led the lamb outside. It cropped happily at the grass by the roadside.

Daylight was breaking over the Judean hills. The last stars were fading in the yellow streaks of sunlight over Jerusalem. The Sabbath was over. Soon Matthew's father would walk to the city to work. His mother and sister would collect water from the well, bake the bread and do the household chores. And he would lead their herd of goats to graze on the hillside.

He was glad he had woken early. There was something he wanted to do on this first day of the week. He wanted to find out where the holy carpenter had been buried. He had been crucified on the Friday, three days before.

Matthew had met him in the village earlier that year when he had been passing through with his disciples. He had healed lame John who had been a cripple from birth, and had told everyone wonderful stories about God. He had even drunk water from *their* family drinking bowl. Later though, things had gone wrong. Cruel men had told lies about him and had got the Roman Governor, Pontius Pilate, to order his execution. Matthew had felt very unhappy that Friday, but he knew he would be less sad if he could find out where the body lay.

He ran steadily along the road to Jerusalem which was about a kilometre and a half away. There were few people about so early in the morning, but ahead of him as he turned a bend, strode a young woman carrying a jar of ointment and some spices in a leather bag. He could smell the spices as he came up behind her and knew by the shape of the jar what it contained. Looking at the red curly hair that escaped from her veil, he recognised her. She was Mary Magdalene, a friend of the carpenter. Surely *she* must know where he was buried. He wouldn't speak to her, though. He knew grown-ups. They often made excuses if a boy asked a question they didn't want to answer. He would follow her and see where she went.

He took great care not to be seen in case she might think that he was a look-out boy for the robbers who hid among the rocks on the mountain-side. Or even that he was a thief himself. Once he threw himself down in a nearby ditch when she looked back and another time he crouched behind a gnarled old olive tree. Nearing the great city more travellers joined them, taking in produce to sell in the market or going to work in the shops and great houses there.

He was right behind Mary as they passed through the city gate.

'Get out of the way!' yelled a man driving a heavily laden cart pulled by a donkey. It rumbled through to the countryside and Matthew had to squeeze into a nearby door-way to avoid being run over.

Next a Roman Centurion, mounted on a white horse, trotted down the narrow street followed by six of his foot-soldiers. Matthew had to stop once more. In the noise and bustle of people moving about in this great city he found that he had lost sight of Mary Magdalene. Tears of disappointment filled his eyes as he realised he couldn't find her in the narrow alleys. He *had* to find her. Then he had to get back before he was missed or his father would whip him. What was he to do? He hated the noise and the crowds, and especially the smell. The city was not sweet like the hillside. Just as he was about to turn for home, he saw the garden.

It was cool under the shade of the trees. He slipped in through the gate. Maybe he could rest and think what to do there. He found himself walking down a sandy path which twisted and turned and before long he could see the city wall once more before him. Soon, right in front of him was a tomb built in the rock. What was strange, though, was that the huge round stone that stopped up the entrance had been rolled away. Who would have done that so early in the morning? It would need several men working together.

As Matthew puzzled over it, he saw her, Mary Magdalene. She had placed her jar of ointment and the package of spices by the dark entrance and was bending her head low to look inside. He crept closer. She was talking to someone unseen. There was a brightness at the back of the cavern above the shelf on which the body should have lain. But there was no body there, just a glimpse of two creatures with wings.

Matthew was very frightened, and he ran a little way back down the path. Yet he *had* to know what it was all about. He hid behind an olive-tree, the feel of its familiar, rough bark comforting him. When he turned to look again at the tomb he saw Mary facing a tall, bearded man dressed in the long white robe of a Rabbi. She was saying urgently:

'If you are the gardener, tell me where he has been laid and I'll take him away.'

Although he could not see the whole of his face, the stranger did not look like a gardener to Matthew. He was trying to remember if he had seen him before when the man uttered one word:

'Mary.'

Immediately, Mary fell at his feet and cried out: 'Master!'

She would have seized hold of his robe, but he said: 'Do not touch me. I have not yet ascended to the Father. But go, tell my brothers that I am returning to the Father, to my God and your God.'

Matthew felt a wonderful happiness in his heart as though he had been given the best present ever, for the man had stepped back and now Matthew could see his face. It was his friend, the holy carpenter, Jesus. In some strange way he was not dead but alive. Matthew wanted to run forward to meet him, but Mary Magdalene came flying down the path and almost knocked him over. When he looked again, Jesus was not there.

Matthew knew that he had to get home and tell his family what had happened, that he had seen Jesus alive. Whether they would believe his story he didn't know, but he just had to tell them. Like Mary, he flew back down the path that first Easter morning, his eyes shining and his face full of glory.

© *Sheila Forsdyke*

Go through the story, introducing the statues, and encouraging the children to tell you anything that they know about the various people. We make a point of mentioning Mary Magdalene as she is the only consistent person at the tomb on Easter Day and deserves a better press than she often gets!

Encourage making connections between the people in this story and those the children have met in other Gospel stories.

Take the statues over to the garden, and retell the story as you (or preferably the children) put the statues in place.

Talk about the feelings on the day – the great sadness – and stress how terrifying the experience of meeting the risen Christ must have been: we're used to the idea of resurrection, they weren't.

Finally, get the children to express how they would have felt when they realized Jesus was alive. Let them cheer and whoop, and you may even get an adult or two joining in!

Easter tableaux

Text

JESUS WAS . . .

BORN

A CHILD

A CARPENTER

A TEACHER

A HEALER

A MIRACLE WORKER

BETRAYED

CRUCIFIED

DEAD

FINISHED

OVER

GONE FOR GOOD . . .

THAT'S WHAT YOU THINK!

Easter drama

(The cast can be all together at the front of the space, or spread around the congregation. If the latter approach is used, it might be advisable to have individuals standing on blocks, pews or chairs to give some height and enable the sound to carry.)

One	You know the tale, you've heard it before
Two	A prisoner brought before the law
Three	Trumped up charges, condemned to death
Four	Finished and done with nothing left.
One	No breath,
Two	No heartbeat,
All	Dead and cold.
Four	A story all too often told.
Three	But . . .
One	On the third day
All	So they say, so they say
Two	When all his followers had
All	Run away, run away
Three	The man they killed was
All	Heard to say, heard to say
One	It is I, who you
All	Put away, put away
One	Risen again on the third day.
All	So they say, so they say.

(The actors reorganize in the space, leaving it clear for Mary and the Angel dancers.)

Four   (*retreating to back of space*) So says Mary Magdalene:

(Mary runs up breathless, perhaps through the audience/congregation.)

Mary   I'm telling you, there was an earthquake. And the stone, rolled away. This shining man, all shining, he rolled it like the stone was nothing at all. And he told us,

Angel   He is not here. He is risen.

Mary   An angel, I tell you it was an angel!

ANGEL DANCE

Mary   An angel, I tell you it was an angel!

Disciple 1   Of course, but it's an idle tale, nothing more.

Four   So said the disciples.

Disciples 1 & 2   An idle tale.

Disciple 3   Let's go.

All   On the road, on the road

Disciple 2   Talking of this and that

Disciple 3   But mostly, mostly of *that*.

All   On the road, on the road

Four   Two travellers, going somewhere . . .

One   Somewhere they don't expect.

Four   On a journey they can't imagine

All   On the road, on the road to Emmaus.

Reader   *Reads Luke 24.15–32*

Congregational song (see p. 67)

Disciples 2 & 3	We have seen the Lord
Four	The disciples said.
Thomas	Not I.
Voices	Not I, Not I.
Thomas	A man came back from the dead?
Alll	Give us a break!
One	A man that can walk through walls?
All	Leave it out!
Two	A ghost of flesh and blood?
All	Give me strength!
Thomas	Give me strength!
Reader	*Reads John 20. 26, 27*

(All clap a slow heartbeat rhythm which gradually increases in volume, continuing under. 'One' steps forward and holds out his arms to silence the heartbeat, the body shape echoing Christ on the cross.)

One	No breath,
All	(*clap, clap*)
Two	No heartbeat,
All	(*clap, clap*)
All	Dead . . . and cold. (*loud clap on 'cold'*)
Four	A story all too often told.

(A silence in which we hear faint whispering, as of secret gossip, then the following voices:)

Mary	An angel, I tell you it was an angel.
Disciples	We have seen the Lord.
Disciple 3	Did not our hearts burn within us?
One	Peace be with you.
Thomas	My Lord and my God.
All	He is risen. Peace be with you.

(All spread out amongst the congregation offering the Peace.)

Congregational song

To the tune of Greensleeves.

We're on the road to Emmaus
Our hearts are heavy within us.
We speak of life, we talk of death
On the road, the road to Emmaus.

Walk, walk along the road
Where Jesus and the disciples trod.
Share, share your lives and thoughts
As you walk the road to Emmaus.

We're walking on the Emmaus road
A stranger offers to share our load.
He speaks of death, he talks of life
On the road, the road to Emmaus.

Walk, walk along the road
Where Jesus and the disciples trod.
Share, share your lives and thoughts
As you walk the road to Emmaus.

At Emmaus we break the bread
Our hearts aflame at what is said.
We talk of death turned to the Life
That we met on the road to Emmaus.

Walk, walk along the road
Where Jesus and the disciples trod.
Share, share your lives and thoughts
As you walk the road to Emmaus.

Easter rap

Everybody shout, shout shout shout
You've heard what the news is all about,
Risen again, let everyone hear
Everybody shout 'cos Easter is here.

Sing it, sing it, sing it out loud
Jesus is risen, tell the crowd,
He's here again, you thought him gone
Sing out loud, sing everyone.

Everybody dance, move to the beat
Jive and skip and tap your feet,
Swing and rumba, dance for joy
Woman, man, girl and boy.

Quiet, hush listen you all
Jesus is back, can you hear him call?
He's here today back from the dead
Listen to what those gospellers said:

He's here, he's back, dead no more
Shout it out from every door,
Sing, dance, he's calling to you
'I rose from the grave, what are you gonna do?'

Rogation

Spring

Summer

Autumn

Winter

Three service and talk outlines

Introduction

Rogation is one of those wonderful festivals that became incorporated into the Christian calendar. We pray for God's blessing on the crops; we 'beat the bounds' (mark the parish boundary with a physical prayer for the crops to grow within it); we do all sorts of things that have little meaning to city-dwelling kids of today. In rural areas, the church was traditionally the focus of the community. The life and health of everybody revolved around the seasons, good weather and a careful stewardship of the land.

Picking up a pre-Christian practice (as ever!) the Church took on board these notions and 'Christianized' them, giving such festivals as Rogation and Harvest. At Rogation the focus is praying for the crops to grow.

The festival is now celebrated by singing songs and psalms around churchyards, by parish walks and other events according to the initiative of the local people – we've heard they've even 'beaten the bounds' in Portsmouth harbour! So here are three ideas for churches everywhere to try and make sense of Rogation. To some they may seem unusual but we encourage you to reclaim an interest in the earth and the creation, and worship God through an increasing awareness of the beauty and miracle around us!

The variety and movement within these services offer a lot that is of interest to the whole family and all-age groups. The first two ideas involve going out into a churchyard if you have one, or a park. The third idea is for an indoor service.

Start both 'outside' services in church with some responses: The Iona worship book *The Pattern of our Days* has some lovely creation-based ideas. Make people aware that today we are to think about the world, the fruitfulness of creation and God's role within that.

Alternatively begin by asking everyone to close their eyes and listen to the sounds around them. After a minute or so ask everyone to say what they heard.

An obvious opening hymn is 'Morning has broken'. We also like 'God is love, His the care'.

We then go out. You have already prayed for a fine day, and have alternatives for if it is tipping it down outside. We have to confess that the twice Ronni has led a Rogation service, it poured the day before, and was glorious on the day itself. Shame about the weddings . . .

Both these services were designed for a church with a wonderful churchyard. A park would do, but burial spaces are essential for the first service.

The Seasons

The first service looks at the cycle of life through focusing on seasons: birth and childhood, adulthood, old age and death.

Spring

Gather everyone at an appropriate point. We used the lych gate – the entrance to the church and grounds, as spring is the entrance of the year.

You could have a short reading from Hildegard of Bingen (ed. Fiona Bowie/Oliver Davies, SPCK 1990). You might also find useful *Beguine Spirituality*, edited and translated by Fiona Bowie/Oliver Davies (SPCK 1989).

Or read the Creation story from Genesis.

After the reading we thought about the spring life coming up – the flowers, nesting birds, the beginnings of life. The thinking was done in a question and answer discussion, with the children providing visual aids as they found them.

Summer

Move to somewhere else to focus on Summer. We went to a formal rose garden, where we focused on the beauty of a tended garden, and how the plants were matured. We also looked at a magnificent horse chestnut and talked about the fruit that would come as a result of the flowers that were there. Again there was a simple question and answer session with the children.

We used a reading from Meister Eckhart, a German theologian of the late middle ages. Not much for the children there so we followed it with the 'Butterfly song' which we sang to a guitar accompaniment. The focus here was on the joys of creation.

Autumn

Move to somewhere which can serve as a focus for growing up and ageing. We settled under a mature tree, and looked at how big things could grow. We also looked for signs of old age creeping up on us and the plants.

There was a reading from Julian of Norwich. During this the younger children were asked to stay close but look around for anything old.

Winter

Find somewhere to focus on the end of life. We stopped at the garden of remembrance, where we inter ashes. The Collect was read, and we talked about the need for bodies to cease, as surely as plants die. We then went on to eternal life, dormant plants rising again, our Easter hope.

Back inside the church we said the closing responses – again from the Iona book. A hymn rounded off the service.

Include the Lord's Prayer in one of the sections – probably in the Autumn.

The Senses

An alternative to the cycle of the seasons is to look at the five senses.

Once again, this was spent mainly around the churchyard, using the plants and any animals that were foolish enough to be passing as visual/sensory aids.

We started with **sight**: read Genesis 1.14–19. Look around – what do you see? Talk about the beauty – maybe share with one person the best thing that you can see, then feed back into the larger group.

Move on, and then at a set place, preferably a good sized tree, explore **touch**: touch some plants, touch some people if you want, then join hands to say the Lord's Prayer quietly and wonderingly.

Move on again, and stop and listen. What can you **hear**? What else have you heard in this area? And so move into a song together, praising God for your senses, for your being.

For the fourth sense, **taste**, we go back into church, where a selection of foods are available – nibbles. Use dried fruits, nuts, biscuits, cheese. Pass them round and enjoy the informal snacking.

The last sense is **smell**. You may wish to burn some incense, and sit and enjoy the smell, rather than using it as an aid to concentrating on something else. Alternatively you could ask people to move around the space, smelling flowers in church. If you have a choir or music group, they could sing or play at this point – a quiet hymn or reflective music. Alternatively play some recorded music. Give the smell time to be appreciated – we rarely savour our sense of smell.

Round off the worship with some prayers and a hymn. You may choose to have a prayer at each of the sense points, thanking God for the sense and remembering those who do not share it.

Both of these outdoor services may well read as very strange. They are no stranger than marching round the church singing psalms! We suggest you walk through the services on your own and then adapt them for your church, and park, or churchyard. Your environs are the focus: use them to pray for God's blessing, and as a focus for thanksgiving.

Talk for Rogation Sunday without a churchyard or with rain!

You need some seedlings, in pots. We used a geranium, a nasturtium and a dwarf bean. If you have a tree seedling use one of those as well.

Start by asking the children who they look like . . . Mum, Dad, but really, everyone is different. Look round – do we have any twins? Are they really the same?

Who's good at . . . ask about various things – trying to include something so that all the children are good at one thing at least.

Get out the plants, one at a time. Ask the children if they know what they are. (Our Brownies were amazingly good at this!) What are the different plants good for? You should get responses that suggest some plants are for looking at – just flowers, apart from the gourmet cooks who eat nasturtium and geranium leaves!; some for eating – beans; and some are trees – what are they for?

Who makes all these plants? God.

Why are they different? Because we'd starve without some for food, and the animals and birds need trees (talk about oxygen if appropriate to age range), and it's lovely to have some just for flowers to look at.

Draw that back to the children – some of us are good at some things, others at different things, but God loves us all.

We had a baptism at this service, so went on to ask who looks after the plants? God and us: we have to water them, and look after them as well. So we need our families to look after us as well as God. We need both families and God to grow up as we should.

Pentecost

Craft, pageant and talk

Introduction

This section takes the well-known story from Acts 2.1–12 and applies it to our own situation. It aims to give a sense of the world-wide nature of the Christian faith and its relevance across national boundaries.

Age range: For making and carrying the placards in procession: any child old enough to carry a simple placard and follow the very simple instructions. Most primary age children will also be able to help with the preparation of the placards.

Reading: Older children/teenagers or adults.

Talk: An experienced worship leader.

Materials: Card, sticks and sticky tape for making 'place name placards'.

Working space: Space in which to prepare the placards – this could happen in Junior Church/Sunday Club prior to the main activity, or it could involve all the church in mixed age groups.

Making the placards

Either in mixed age groups or Junior Church/Sunday Club, create placards by attaching a piece of card to a stick (garden canes are ideal). The placard should be large enough for what is to be written on it to be read from the back of the church.

On one side of each placard, one of the place names from the reading should be written in big bold letters:

PARTHIA, MEDIA, ELAM, MESOPOTAMIA, JUDAEA, CAPPADOCIA, PONTUS, ASIA, PHRYGIA, PAMPHYLIA, EGYPT, LIBYA, CRETE, ARABIA.

Give the easier 4/5 letter names to the younger children and ensure that everyone has a clearly written example to copy from.

On the reverse side of the placards, ask the participants to write down places that they know or know of. You will end up with, for example, a placard with CRETE on one side and DERBY on the other, or perhaps one side will read PONTUS and the other INDIA. The reverse of some placards should be really local with area or even street names from your locality.

Pageant

This takes place all together in church. Prime the children who will be carrying the placards to ensure that only the side with the biblical place name faces forward (perhaps they could be colour coded so that you could ask for only the red side to face forward).

The reading begins – read by an adult, older teenager, or split amongst a group. As the different place names are mentioned, the children enter one at a time, on cue, holding their placards high. For a more dramatic interpretation the reader could pronounce each name as if announcing teams at the Olympic Games and the congregation could be encouraged to cheer and clap.

When the reading is finished the worship leader could move amongst the group briefly explaining the importance of the message for all these people from different places, stressing that the message was 'right for them' whatever their background. The talk should be short and to the point – remember the tired arms of the placard holders.

The next stage is for the children to turn their placards round and process around the building so that everyone can see what's written on them – you might do this during a hymn or have some other music at this point.

Pentecost talk

This follows on from the pageant.

The children return to the front and the worship leader talks about the importance of the Apostles' message for our world, our country, our area, our streets – in each case indicating appropriate placards. You can use a question and answer technique and record the answers on a flip chart for use in the prayers:

What would we like the Holy Spirit to do in our world.

How can we join in the task(s)?

Move through the various areas, becoming more specific as you get closer to home. The final point is that the relevance is for us – at which point a placard with the name of the church on it is produced.

Pentecost rap

Introduction

Like all the raps in this book, the example on page 78 one can be rehearsed by children in their own session and then presented to the whole church when everyone joins together. It can also be used as a basis for children writing their own raps. Aim for a sharp, clear delivery. To maintain interest, if you have a large enough group, you could split the verses between smaller groups or give lines such as Peter's and the crowd's to individuals. You could also use a rhythm backing from a tape or keyboard.

Age range:	7–12. The age range will depend on how the idea is developed; teenagers might like to perform their own raps with accompaniment.
Working space:	Space in which to prepare away from the main church – could be quite noisy!

Pentecost rap

Who's that crowd?
What's the fuss?
A noise, commotion, a bubbling buzz.

'They look drunk'
A voice calls out
And other voices heckle and shout.

A guy called Peter stands up tall
Calls for order,
'Gonna tell you all.
These folks aren't drunk as you suppose
The work of God just grows and grows.
We are sinners, we've done wrong
But now we sing a different song.'

He tells of his boss from Galilee
Jesus, who set Peter free.
A man who died and rose again
And sends his spirit on women and men.
His Holy Spirit for one and all
So said Peter when he stood up tall.

Summer

Summer School

Introduction

Many churches run some kind of Summer School or holiday activity during the school break. A full exposition of such schemes demands a book of its own and there are many different possible patterns.

Our approach has been to run Arts Workshops for about twenty children taking a different Bible theme each year. One year we ran *The Arks Workshop*, taking Noah's ark as a starting point for looking at creation and ecology. Another year's theme was *Lost Kids*, looking at the Prodigal Son; the *Sowing Seeds Workshop* looked at the parable of the Sower.

Outline

The format each year was roughly the same:

> Age range 7–11
>
> Two hours each morning from 10.00 to 12.00

+ The first fifteen minutes were spent looking at the story and discussing it.

+ The next thirty minutes were for drama games and getting to know you games – fun stuff!

+ Then came a break for a drink and biscuit.

+ The next fifty minutes were led by a guest arts workshop leader – sometimes Gordon or Ronni, but often a musician, painter, dancer . . .

+ Ten minutes were needed to cool down, round up and recap.

Each year these attracted local radio reporters (always desperate for something lively and different!), and each year the interviewer clearly felt that, fun and engaging though it all was, there was a certain lack of plain teaching – so you'll gather that these were not evangelistic summer schools in the usual sense. Our focus was on exploring the story and inviting children into the church, encouraging them to use and develop their skills and abilities. We suspect, perhaps arrogantly, that the act of creating and expressing together will stay with these children a long time and will bear fruit later.

We were very fortunate to have a number of people with church connections who were prepared to lead workshops, but this is not essential. Many of the ideas in this book could be used, adapted and developed. One approach would be to tell the story of Jesus' life through the week, using ideas in the following way.

Monday
Jesus is born

Work on one of the Christmas plays from this book. Or tell the Christmas story using still pictures and narration.

Alternatively work on the Christmas rap on page 19 – and/or develop your own.

Craft. Make pictures like Advent calendars with four or five inns with opening doors. Each door has an innkeeper behind saying, 'No room'. Double doors open on to a stable scene.

Tuesday
Jesus is dedicated

Use the Candlemas ideas on pages 40–42 as a starting point.

Activities could include candle making/decorating.

Drawing/writing prayers (see page 42).

Talking about the next part of the story in Luke, where Jesus' parents lose him – have the children ever been lost, what happened, what did it feel like?

Wednesday
Jesus starts work

The Parable of the Two House Builders on pages 84–7. Use this drama to illustrate Jesus' use of parables.

Read and then rehearse the play, which is quite simple (children can hold their scripts as they work).

Craft. Tell the story of a a parable in comic strip form – see Easter pew sheet for ideas.

Thursday
Easter

Use the Easter Tableaux ideas on pages 56–7 and 63.

And/or use the rap ideas on pages 59 and 68.

Craft. Make Easter gardens or wax and wash paintings using the dark colours of the crucifixion and the brilliant light of the resurrection.

Friday
The Holy Spirit

Work on the Pentecost rap on pages 77–8.

Raps could run through the week with a new one each day.

You could end the week with a performance of some of the work.

Craft: Use the craft and pageant ideas in Pentecost (see pages 76–7).

The week could be called *The Gospel Rap* or *Lifeweek* or *Matthew, Mark, Luke and Art*.

Games

The following games would be good as fun starters to each day.

Monday

Christmas presents

The whole group sit on chairs in a circle. You need a fairly large circle with space to run around in the middle. The leader has no chair and stands in the middle.

Give each person one of four names of Christmas presents – socks, chocolates, hankies, shampoo. Ask them to remember what they are.

You call out one of the categories and those people must stand up, find a new chair and sit down again. You will also be looking for a chair and if you find one, there will be a different person in the middle who calls out a category.

If they choose, the person in the middle may call 'Christmas Day', at which everyone has to find a new seat.

Tuesday

Put out the candle

A version of 'wink murder', unsubtly adapted to fit the theme!

The group stand in a circle. One person is chosen to leave the room. While that person is out choose someone to be the 'breeze'. The rest of the group are 'candles'.

Invite the 'guesser' back into the room. They stand in the centre of the circle and say,

'Breeze blow, candle flame go.'

The 'breeze' may now blow out three candles by winking at them. If winked at a candle must 'go out' by sitting down. After three candles are 'out' the guesser must try to guess who is the breeze. If they get it wrong they say again, 'Breeze blow, candle flame go,' and the game continues for another three 'hits'.

It may continue like this until there are only the guesser and one or two others left standing.

Wednesday

Story telling

There are a number of games where a group make up a story, telling it around a circle.

They may do this –

- one sentence at a time;

- one word at a time;

- one sentence at a time with each starting alternately 'Fortunately' and 'Unfortunately';

- going once round the circle and having to include three diverse objects in the same story, such as a book, a moon rocket, a lettuce leaf . . .

They can also play an alphabet word game, going round the circle and taking a letter of the alphabet each to complete the sentence:

'I went to the moon and it was . . .' Amazing, beautiful, cold, dreary, entirely boring . . .

Thursday

Hiding

The whole group stand in their own space. Ask each person to think of someone in the room. They should not look at the chosen person or indicate in any way who they have chosen. Tell them to remember that this person is a Roman.

Now ask them to think of someone else – again they do not indicate their choice. Tell them that this person is a rock.

Now explain that they are followers of Jesus who want to hide from Romans. When you say go, everyone must move so that their rock is between themselves and their Roman. Everyone moves at once and the resulting chaos is great fun. Sometimes (very occasionally) the whole thing comes to rest with everyone in the 'right' place, but usually it just keeps going until you call a halt.

Friday

In the crowd

Prepare four sets of different coloured stickers that everyone can wear on their foreheads. Stick them in position without anyone seeing their own colour.

When you say go, everyone has to find their fellow colours and sit together in their colour group *without talking* or touching. They will quickly realize that this can only happen when individuals work together.

There is a range of holiday club material on the market, such as Scripture Union's *Scrap Happy, Newshounds* and *Shipshapes*. Also worth a look are Steve Pearce and Diana Murrie's book *All Aboard!* (NCEC, 1996) and Claire Gibbs' *Building New Bridges* (NS/CHP, 1996).

The Parable of the Two House Builders

Introduction

This is a simple drama which can be read at microphones, requiring a minimum of movement. It is ideal for churches with poor sight lines. Its 'sand' theme offers a tenuous link with summer and it could form part of a Summer School (see page 78). The script can be found on pages 83–5.

Taking the well-known Parable of the Two Builders, this piece would work well as a replacement for the Gospel reading. It was first performed at St Alban's Church, Hemel Hempstead, in August 1996, with a mixture of primary age, secondary age and adult. There was one rehearsal the Saturday before the Sunday service.

Age range:	This is a genuine all age script, suitable for primary age readers right up to adult. Very young children could join in the 'All' lines.
Working space:	The performance space can be quite small since there is little movement.

Production notes

Aim for a fast paced performance.

Simple movement will help:

'*Brick by brick, block by block*'

— build one fist upon another as in the song, 'The wise man built . . .'

'*Look at the clouds, Look at the sky, Storm's a coming*'

— exaggerated shielding eyes and pointing

'*This way, That way, This way, That way*'

— whole cast sways

The Parable of the Two House Builders

Script

One	Mr
Two	And Mrs
One & Two	Wise
Three	Decided to build a house.
One & Two	We've made a plan, we've got a scheme For the finest house you've ever seen –
One	Windows, doors, walls and roof,
Two	Snug and warm and weatherproof.
Three	Only one question remained –
One & Two	Where, oh where to build.
One	Here?
Two	Or here?
One	There?
Two	Or there?
One & Two	Where, oh where?
All	THERE!
One	Looks solid.
Two	Looks tough.
One	Looks strong enough.
Two	A nice firm rock on which to build.
Three	And so they built their house:
All	Brick by brick, block by block Build it tall and finally STOP.

Three	And have a party.
All	Yippee, hooray (*etc.*)

(*Party sounds and movement. This would be a good opportunity to rearrange positions so that Four and Five take the places of One and Two.*)

Four	Mr
Five	And Mrs
Four & Five	Fool
Three	Decided to build a house.
Four & Five	We've made a plan, we've got a scheme For the finest house you've ever seen –
Four	Windows, doors, walls and roof,
Five	Snug and warm and weatherproof.
Three	Only one question remained –
Four & Five	Where, oh where to build.
Four	Here?
Five	Or here?
Four	There?
Five	Or there?
Four & Five	Where, oh where?
All	THERE!
Four	Looks cool.
Five	Looks grand.
Four	And the kids can play on that lovely sand.
Three	And so they built their house:
All	Brick by brick, block by block Build it tall and finally STOP.
Three	And have a party.
All	Yippee, hooray (*etc.*)
Three	Hold it!

One	Look at the clouds
Two	Look at the sky
Three	Storm's a coming
All	My oh my!
Four	Close the windows
Five	Seal the doors
One	Stay inside
Two	While it pours.
Three	And it rained
All	Pitter patter, pitter patter
Three	And the wind blew
All	Gust, gust, flying dust
Three	The rivers rose
All	Up up, up up, up and over.
Three	And the house on the rock went –
One	Creak, creak. I'm fine.
Three	And the house on the sand went –
All	This way That way This way That way.
Four	Oh no!
Five	Oh my!
Four	My house!
All	GOODBYE. (*All clap*)
Three	And the house on the sand fell flat.

Harvest

The Parable of the Talents

Introduction

This is another simple script to be read or learnt (see pp. 93–4). It was first performed by the Sunday School at St Peter's Church, St Albans, in July 1995. There was one practice the week before, and a quick run-through before the service.

Age range: Primary age children and older, up to adult. Young children, or those who don't wish to speak out loud individually can join in the simple 'All' lines.

Working space: Space to practise away from the rest of the congregation. The performance space can be quite small since there is no movement. This makes it ideal for a church with poor sight lines (how many fit that category!). The play works very well as a rehearsed reading performed at microphones.

The Parable of the Sower

Introduction

This very simple drama uses a well-known and popular format – the retelling of a parable with exaggerated comic mime (see pp. 95–6). The piece is designed to be worked on by the Sunday Club and then performed in church immediately afterwards. We give two versions on the photocopy sheets. One is for rehearsal and contains all the directions for the mime, the other gives just the words – useful for the Narrator during a performance.

Age range: This is suitable for a wide age range. This version was performed at St Peter's Church, St Albans with primary age children and one adult. There is one Narrator and everyone else works together as a kind of chorus.

Working space: Enough room for drama with the children/young people. Performance space – with as good a view as possible for the congregation.

Harvest song

To the tune of 'Here we go round the mulberry bush'.

Simple actions can be added to each verse. The line 'Thank you God for the harvest' can be accompanied by uplifted arms in praise, followed by a gathering-in movement.

In addition:

v. 1   Simple harvesting movements – wide sweeps as with a traditional scythe.

v. 2   Picking movements as in harvesting nuts and fruits.

v. 3   Draw a square in the air for boxes. Open one hand for bags, twist the other hand (as if using a can opener) for cans. This is quite hard so be prepared for some fun as everyone tries to get the hang of it!

v. 4   Large encircling gestures.

v. 5   Point to yourself and others.

Harvest rap

Introduction

Like all the raps in this book, the example on page 98 can be rehearsed by children in their own session and then presented to the whole church when everyone joins together. It can also be used as a basis for children writing their own raps. Aim for a sharp, clear delivery. To maintain interest, if you have a large enough group, you could split the verses between smaller groups. You could also use a rhythm backing from a tape or keyboard.

This rap is in two halves which could be two different groups, one after the other, or you could put each half either side of a talk.

Age range: 7–12. The age range will depend on how the idea is developed; teenagers might like to perform their own raps with accompaniment.

Working space: Space in which to prepare away from the main church – could be quite noisy!

Harvest talk

This is a very simple talk which uses visual aids to focus on God's love for us as expressed through Harvest.

You will need:

- ◆ conkers
- ◆ compost
- ◆ some plant pots
- ◆ water
- ◆ a hairdryer.

Gather the children near the front or, if appropriate, the whole talk could happen outside.

Show the conkers and ask:

> Where do they come from?
>
> What do they become?
>
> What do seeds need if they are to grow?

Warmth, Water, Time, Food.

Talk about how the seeds obtain these things, and get the children to plant a conker during the following. If you have more than two or three doing this you'll need some assistants, and a great deal of floor protection if inside!

Where does the food come from? The soil – put soil in the pots. Then put in a conker.

Where does the water come from? It rains – so water the compost.

Where does the warmth come from? The sun, so get out that hairdryer! (not needed if outside)

Why aren't they growing now? Because they need time.

What do people need to make them grow?

People need four things to let them grow too – Food, Water, Time, and Love.

Where does our food come from? Indicate the harvest produce, and remind the congregation that many of these items were brought from outside the UK.

Where does our water come from? Remind folks of the need to be careful with our water.

Where does love come from? From our families and from God.

And what about time? Do we give ourselves time, on our own, and together, to grow?

So thank God that all the things that we need to grow come from him.

The Parable of the Talents

Script

One   The Kingdom of Heaven is like a boss who is going on a journey

Two   So all the servants get called together.

One   To receive gifts of money, called talents.

Three   One servant gets five talents. Yippee!

Four   Another gets two talents. Yippee – ish.

Two   The third servant gets one talent. Great.

One   And off goes the boss on the journey.

All   Goodbyeeeeeeee!

Three   The one who had five talents got busy.

All   Busy, busy, busy, busy.

Three   And in no time at all had made five more talents.

All   Yippeee.

Four   The one who had two talents got busy.

All   Busy, busy, busy, busy.

Four   And in no time at all had made two more talents.

All   Yippeee.

Two   The servant who had one talent also got busy.

All   Busy, busy, busy, busy.

Two	Got busy digging a hole.
All	Dig, dig, diggity dig.
Two	And buried the talent.
All	Goodbyeee!
One	After a long time the boss came back.
All	Hello boss!
Three	The one who had five talents brought forth the five talents more.
One	Well done, have a bun, all my praise you have won.
Four	The one who had two talents brought forth the two talents more.
One	Well done, have a bun, all my praise you have won.
Two	Then the servant who had buried his one talent stepped forward.
One	Well now chum, will you have a bun, are my praises truly won?
Two	The thing is boss . . . I know you're a rotten poet, and a hard boss so I . . . hid my talent in the ground.
All	Dig, dig, hid, hid, in the ground where it can't be found.
One	And you call me a rotten poet. You lazy good-for-nothing servant. Dig up his talent and give it to the others. Throw him to the outer darkness.
All	Send him to (*add name of local landmark!*)
One	So off he went, talent-less, while the rest had a marvellous party.
All	To all those who have will more be given. Dig, dig, diggity dig. Goodbyeeee.

The Parable of the Sower

Script with actions

(All enter and stand at the rear of the area with their backs to the congregation. At a signal from the leader, all turn with fingers on lips.)

All   Shhhh. Listen!

Narrator   Once there was a man who went out to sew his socks.

All   No, no, listen, you've got it wrong. *(etc.)*

Narrator   Once there was a man who went out to sow corn. As he scattered the seed in the field, some of it fell along the path and the birds came and ate it up.

(All (except Narrator) become birds swooping around the space and pecking up the seeds.)

Some of it fell on rocky ground where there was little soil. The seeds soon sprouted because the soil wasn't deep. Then when the sun came up it burnt the young plants; and because the roots had not grown deep enough the plants soon dried up.

(All (except Narrator) show signs of intense heat, mopping brows, wilting etc. Eventually flop over (bending at the hips) with a sigh.)

Some of the seed fell among thorn bushes, which grew up and choked the plants, and they didn't produce any corn.

(All stand again. Some mime choking others. This will be safest, and look best, if taller people stand behind shorter and mime a squeezing action without actually making contact. The strangled plants become weaker and weaker until they flop as before. Those who did the choking rub their hands with glee.)

But some seed fell in good soil, and the plants sprouted, grew and produced corn: some had thirty grains, others sixty and others a hundred.

(All sit during the above. Then a few stand on 'thirty grains', more on 'sixty', and all on 'a hundred'. They should stand tall and proud as if posing for a group photo.)

Narrator   Listen.

All   Listen, if you have ears.

(All freeze.)

(Good News Bible)

The Parable of the Sower

Script without actions

All   Shhhh. Listen!

Narrator   Once there was a man who went out to sew his socks.

All   No, no, listen, you've got it wrong. (*etc.*)

Narrator   Once there was a man who went out to sow corn. As he scattered the seed in the field, some of it fell along the path and the birds came and ate it up.

Some of it fell on rocky ground where there was little soil. The seeds soon sprouted because the soil wasn't deep. Then when the sun came up it burnt the young plants; and because the roots had not grown deep enough the plants soon dried up.

Some of the seed fell among thorn bushes, which grew up and choked the plants, and they didn't produce any corn.

But some seed fell in good soil, and the plants sprouted, grew and produced corn: some had thirty grains, others sixty and others a hundred.

Listen.

All   Listen, if you have ears.

(*Good News Bible*)

Harvest song

To the tune of Here we go round the mulberry bush

Harvest time is here again
Here again, here again
Harvest time is here again
Thank you God for the harvest.

Fruits and nuts and pulses and grains
Pulses and grains, pulses and grains
Fruits and nuts and pulses and grains
Thank you God for the harvest.

Food in boxes and bags and cans
Bags and cans, bags and cans
Food in boxes and bags and cans
Thank you God for the harvest.

For all the colours and kinds of food
Kinds of food, kinds of food
For all the colours and kinds of food
Thank you God for the harvest.

For all the things that we can do
We can do, me and you can do
For all the things that we can do
We thank you God of the Harvest.

Harvest rap

Group One:

What does Harvest mean, yeah?
What's this all about?
Don't want to seem mean, yeah?
But we're having serious doubts.
You see we don't plough and scatter
We don't grow any seeds.
The fish we eat is battered
We don't put out to sea.
So what's this festival for, yeah?
What's the reason why?
Harvest could be a bore, yeah?
The thing just don't apply.

Group Two:

We hear what you are saying
But don't you ever think?
Someone does the growing
To make your food and drink.
It doesn't grow in boxes
In a supermarket store.
It's not shrink-wrapped in nature
So what is Harvest for?
To say a great big thank you
For everything we share
To think of hungry people,
Try to make the world more fair.

Remembrance

Remembrance prayers

Introduction

Remembrance services can be particularly difficult for children and they must rank amongst those at which adults most resent noise and bustle. With these factors in mind, this very simple spoken piece (see pp. 102–3) is designed to be created in Sunday Club/Junior Church and then shared with the whole church at, or towards, the end of the service.

This was first used at a Remembrance service at St Peter's Church, Gadebridge, Hemel Hempstead. The participants were mostly Brownies and Cubs (older uniformed organizations being elsewhere). We provided the start of the piece in scripted form and used the children's ideas to complete it. Its simple, solemn approach was entirely in keeping with the service, yet gave a real focus for the children.

Age range:	Primary age children and older. Most do not need to be able to read aloud, but a handful should have clear, loud voices and be able to read/learn a simple sentence.
Materials:	Scripts – either complete or half finished. Paper, pens/pencils.
Working space:	A space away from the rest of the congregation in which to practise (the rehearsal time might be quite loud).

Practice

Begin by talking about the children's understanding of Remembrance Sunday, and in particular their ideas of why we remember.

It would be useful to have some items on hand to act as discussion starters – a medal, picture of war graves, picture of victory celebrations, for example. If appropriate to your group, you could ask them to close their eyes and think about any wars that they have heard of, either in the past or in recent times. When they open their eyes they can discuss these and you could draw out a list of words related to the theme.

Hand out the half-finished scripts, and practise everyone saying, 'Remember, remember, remember'. Aim for clarity with everyone speaking together. Conduct this so that everyone comes in at the same time.

Share out the other lines on the script (the speakers' names are left blank on the photocopy master). Lines can be shared with two or more children speaking in unison in order to involve more.

Practise the whole piece several times, then break to talk about what can go after, 'We remember because . . .' Aim for pithy short statements based on ideas from the earlier discussion — those suggested by the Gadebridge group are given in the second version of the script.

Once you have chosen the words, allocate these lines.

Aim for a couple of full runs-through with full projection and everyone standing where they can see the conductor. Practise getting up from pews (or entering from Sunday Club) and sitting again at the end. The conductor should signal these.

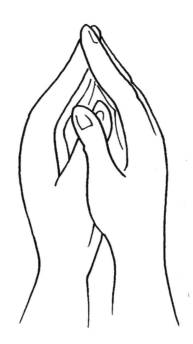

Remembrance prayers

Script

Version 1 with gaps

All   Remember, remember, remember
Those who fought in two world wars
The injured and all who died

All   Remember, remember, remember
Remember the Falklands
Northern Ireland
Bosnia
Zaire

All   Remember, remember, remember
Remember all who mourn and weep

All   Remember, remember, remember
Why do we remember?
We remember because . . .
(*add children's ideas and end with:*)

All   Remember, remember, remember.

Remembrance prayers

Script

Version 2 with ideas from St Peter's, Gadebridge

All	Remember, remember, remember
1.	Those who fought in two world wars
2.	The injured and all who died
All	Remember, remember, remember
3.	Remember the Falklands
4.	Northern Ireland
5.	Bosnia
6.	Zaire
All	Remember, remember, remember
7.	Remember all who mourn and weep
All	Remember, remember, remember
8.	Why do we remember?
9.	We remember because . . .
10.	They gave their lives for us
11.	People risked their lives to save us
12.	We can pray for them
13.	And their families and friends
All	Remember, remember, remember.

Pew sheets

Introduction

Pew sheets can extend the range of activities from speaking and listening to drawing and writing – and of course the concomitant thinking and feeling. There is a danger that they are used merely to keep children quiet while the adults get on with the serious business of worship. Realistically very few pencil and paper activities will keep all the children quiet for all the time. Some will find the activities inappropriate, others will require and request help, others might be so excited by their work that they simply have to tell the adults all about it, NOW!

For these reasons, pew sheets should be used sparingly. We believe that they are most useful when seen as an extension of the teaching and exploration of worship, rather than as a means to providing peace and quiet.

Pew sheets can be used in church as a quiet activity, or the children can use them in their own Sunday Club type session. The latter is educationally stronger because it allows for discussion and more sharing of ideas. On the other hand there is a lot to be said for encouraging the notion that worship can involve different groups working side by side on different things but absorbing some of what each other is doing. If they are used in this way this can either be where the children sit (literally in the pew in some cases), or in a special children's area at the back or side of the church. In some churches children kneel on kneelers, resting their work on a pew or chair. Exactly how pew sheets are used will depend on physical and practical factors as much as spiritual.

If you can, make up packs containing the relevant sheet(s) for the service, extra plain sheets and a selection of pencils and colours. A zip-up plastic folder makes an ideal container and gives an impression that this is something of value.

Most of the sheets have a creative focus, but they also include puzzles and games to give them a wider appeal. Although you may find just what you want in what we offer, it is more likely that you will want to create your own sheets, focusing more closely on the needs of your children in terms of age, temperament and ability, and on the specific focus of your worship. You can cut up copies of our offerings to create your own sheets with some of our ideas and some of your own, or simply use our sheets for inspiration – if only in the form of 'I can do better than that'!

Whatever sheets you use, we make a plea for them to be integrated into the worship:

✦ Give them out at an appropriate time and make something of this – they are as important as any part of the worship.

✦ Link them thematically to what has gone before and what will follow.

✦ Refer to them later and look at the results as part of the service.

✦ Invite the congregation to look at the work after the service and talk about it with the children.

Contents

The following sheets are provided: all will need pencils and colours, and some might require extra plain sheets as well.

Advent / Christmas 1

A pew sheet on the theme of waiting for Christmas, linking our wait for the 'great day' with Mary and Joseph waiting for the birth of their baby. Use in the run-up to Christmas Day.

Advent / Christmas 2

A sheet for use on Christmas Day, taking the theme of celebration and gifts.

Candlemas

An outline picture specifically for use with the Candlemas Service outline on pages 40–42.

Families 1 and 2

Two sheets with activities for services focusing on the family, such as Mothering Sunday.

Easter 1 and 2

Drawing, writing and puzzle activity focusing on the Easter story.

Pentecost 1 and 2

Sheets which aid recall around the events of Pentecost. For the Wordsearch we encourage you to ask the children to call out their results as part of the service.

Harvest 1 and 2

Ideas for prayers and thinking about Harvest.

One final thought on pew sheets

Occasionally give the adults a pack of things to do while the worship focuses on the needs of children!

Advent/Christmas 1

Colour in the picture.

Who are these two people?

M _ _ _ and J _ _ _ _ _

What are they waiting for?
Write or draw your answer here

Can you guide Mary and Joseph to the right Inn?

On the back of this sheet or on another sheet, draw a picture of something you're waiting for at Christmas. It might be a present, a party, food or fun with your family and friends.

Advent/Christmas 2

On the back of this sheet design a poster to invite people to come to Church this Christmas. What will your message be? You could use one of the ideas below or make up your own. Then draw a bright, lively picture on your poster.

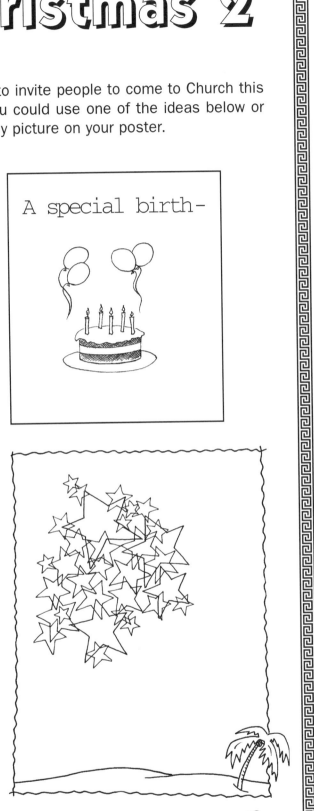

a	n	g	e	l	l	j
c	f	p	f	i	n	e
h	o	r	c	u	t	s
r	f	s	i	n	n	u
i	b	a	y	e	t	s
s	a	c	m	a	n	r
t	b	r	a	i	l	d
m	y	i	z	o	l	t
a	x	b	t	s	u	y
s	t	a	r	p	r	b

Find the following Christmas words in this wordsearch:

family   angel   star   friend   crib
christmas   jesus   fun   baby

How many stars can you count?

Who followed a star to find Jesus?

Add them to the picture above

Candlemas

Families 1

Write a prayer for someone in your family. Draw a picture of the person in the box and then complete the prayer next to it. If you want to write or draw a longer prayer you can do it on the back of this sheet. You could ask God to help them in some way or tell God what you really like about them.

This is _____.

Thank you God for

_____.

Amen.

How many people can you see in Church? On another sheet, draw a smiley face for everyone whose name you know.

Families 2

I can't make up my mind

Hello Mum!

Get there fast!

I like a good laugh

Let's dance

I can't wait to find out what happens

Everyone is different. Draw lines to match each family member to what they say.

On the back of this sheet draw a picture of yourself and write a sentence which describes what you are like.

Put the words of this prayer in the right order and then add your own last line:

especially my family.

to help them.

Thank you for everyone,

Please help me

Dear God,

And I pray especially for . . .

Easter 1

Gloomy days and shouts of praise

1.   **2.**   **3.**

1. **The followers of Jesus were sad when he was killed – draw a sad face.**

2. **They were puzzled when Mary said Jesus was alive again – draw a puzzled face.**

3. **They were happy when they met Jesus risen from the dead – draw a happy face.**

What might Jesus' friends have said when they saw him alive again? Can you unscramble these words?

JSESU SI LAVIE _ _ _ _ _ _ _ _ _ _ _ _

RAYHOO _ _ _ _ _ _

MAZANIG _ _ _ _ _ _ _

EH SI RISNE _ _ _ _ _ _ _ _ _

On the back of this page or on a separate sheet, make a newspaper front page telling the story of Jesus coming back to life. You'll need a headline, a short written story and an exciting picture.

Easter 2

Easter – the true story

Draw the story of Jesus dying and then coming back to life as an exciting, colourful comic strip – use the spaces below for each picture. We've started the first one for you.

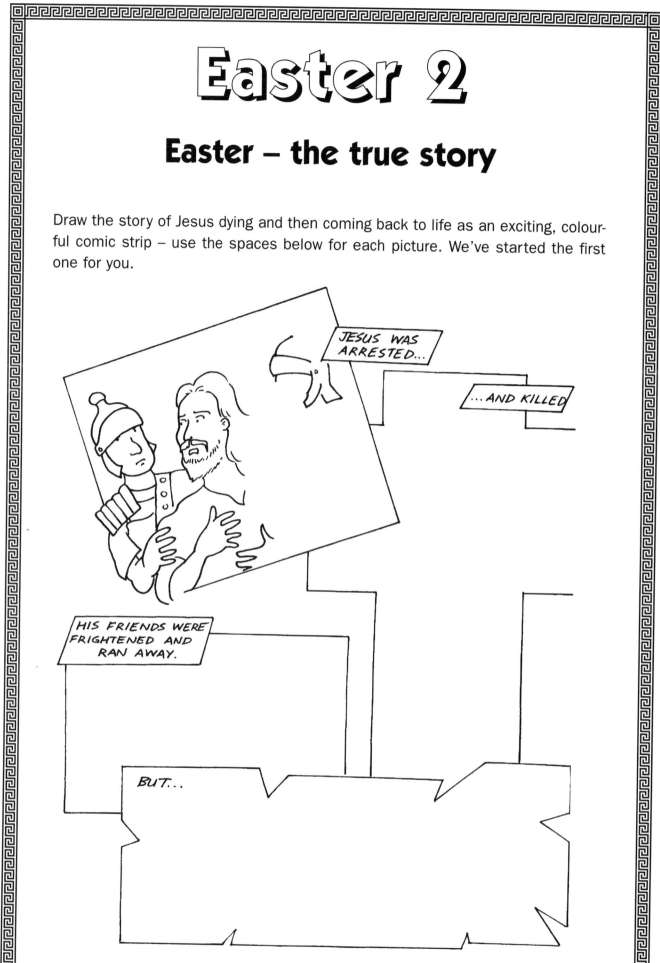

Pentecost 1

What happened at Pentecost? The story is told in a book of the Bible called The Acts of the Apostles.

Draw or write your answer here:

What special gift did God give at Pentecost?

Fill in the missing letters: _ h _   H _ _ _   S _ _ _ _ _ _

On the back or on a separate sheet draw your idea of what the Holy Spirit looks like.

Pentecost 2

Find some words from the story of Pentecost in this wordsearch:

t	a	c	t	s	r	w	i	n	d
h	o	l	y	s	p	i	r	i	t
c	p	k	g	q	u	p	l	o	n
r	h	o	k	o	d	e	s	p	i
o	f	t	w	f	d	o	h	e	d
w	i	i	s	e	h	p	y	r	o
d	r	n	q	o	r	i	n	e	v
c	e	t	r	y	l	e	p	r	e

holy spirit   **dove**

fire   **crowd**

god   **wind**

acts   **people**

peter   **power**

Everyone watching was amazed to see how lively and excited the followers of Jesus were. Can you write what some of the crowd might have said?

Harvest 1

Harvest prayers

Write a thank you prayer, thanking God for all we have to eat.

On a separate sheet write a prayer for people around the world who don't have enough food or have no choice about what they eat. Colour the borders around your prayers.

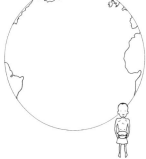

Harvest 2

Make a 'Happy Harvest' card.

Draw a harvest picture for the front of the card.

Inside you can write a special Harvest message like:

**Happy Harvest   Thank God for food
Harvest time is here again**

You could decorate your card with pictures cut from magazines and catalogues.

Who will you send your card to?

Can you find the way to the food?

On a separate sheet or on the back of this one, draw around your hand. Then colour each finger a different colour and turn each one into a picture of a tree or plant growing out of the world.